The Mysterious & Unknown

The Bermuda Triangle

by Gail B. Stewart

ReferencePoint Press™

San Diego, CA

©2009 ReferencePoint Press, Inc.

For more information, contact:
ReferencePoint Press, Inc.
PO Box 27779
San Diego, CA 92198
www.ReferencePointPress.com

Picture credits:
cover: istockphoto.com
AP Images: 17, 25, 28–29, 32–33, 39, 64, 90, 91
Joe Bernier: 8, 49
Istockphoto.com: 11, 87
Photoshot: 62–63
North Wind: 13
Science Photo Library: 44, 58–59, 58 (inset), 66, 70–71, 82–83

Series design and book layout:
Amy Stirnkorb

LIBRARY OF CONGRESS CATALOGING-IN-PUBLICATION DATA

Stewart, Gail B. (Gail Barbara), 1949-
  The Bermuda Triangle / by Gail B. Stewart.
      p. cm. -- (The mysterious & unknown)
  Includes bibliographical references and index.

  ISBN-13: 978-1-60152-056-2 (hardback)
  ISBN-10: 1-60152-056-5 (hardback)
  1. Bermuda Triangle--Juvenile literature. I. Title.
  G558.S74 2008

001.94--dc22   2008040860

CONTENTS

FOREWORD

"Strange is our situation here upon earth."
—Albert Einstein

Since the beginning of recorded history, people have been perplexed, fascinated, and even terrified by events that defy explanation. While science has demystified many of these events, such as volcanic eruptions and lunar eclipses, some remain outside the scope of the provable. Do UFOs exist? Are people abducted by aliens? Can some people see into the future? These questions and many more continue to puzzle, intrigue, and confound despite the enormous advances of modern science and technology.

It is these questions, phenomena, and oddities that Reference-Point Press's *The Mysterious & Unknown* series is committed to exploring. Each volume examines historical and anecdotal evidence as well as the most recent theories surrounding the topic in debate. Fascinating primary source quotes from scientists, experts, and eyewitnesses as well as in-depth sidebars further inform the text. Full-color illustrations and photos add to each book's visual appeal. Finally, source notes, a bibliography, and a thorough index provide further reference and research support. Whether for research or the curious reader, *The Mysterious & Unknown* series is certain to satisfy those fascinated by the unexplained.

INTRODUCTION

Without a Trace

The stories are bizarre, and while they differ in the details, they all share a thread of similarity. A plane is flying over the Atlantic, east or south of Florida. The weather is usually clear, with no sign of storms or even clouds. But without warning, there are problems. In the cockpit, compasses, altimeters, and other navigational instruments—often millions of dollars' worth—go haywire, spinning crazily. Pilots frantically radio for help, trying to explain that they can no longer see and have no idea where they are. The sky, which moments ago had been a brilliant blue, has become an odd, milky color.

Air controllers on the ground, tracking planes with radar, watch as the blip on their screen that corresponds to that plane suddenly disappears. As rescue planes and ships speed to the area where the plane is believed to have gone down, they are stunned to find nothing. There is no wreckage, no sign of bodies—not even an oil slick that could give searchers a location of a crash at sea. Even in the weeks and months afterward, nothing is washed up on shore. It is as if the plane—as well as its crew and passengers—never existed.

Disappearances

It is true, of course, that planes and ships can experience trouble and subsequently go missing anywhere. But this particular section of the Atlantic Ocean has seen such occurrences on a frighteningly large scale—far more than any other region of the earth's oceans. Stories about strange disappearances have circulated for more than 500 years, long before official records were kept, so there is no way of knowing how many people have been lost in that area. However, in the 30 years between 1945 and 1975, 67 boats, and at least 192 aircraft of all types—as well as 1,700 people—have vanished there. And since 1975, an average of 20 boats and 4 aircraft disappear there each year. Not all of the losses are small boats or planes. Large ships—some as large as 19,000 tons (17,237 metric tons), have disappeared. Commercial airliners and even an entire squadron of U.S. Navy bombers have vanished, too.

As puzzling as the large number of disappearances is the specific location of the events. For example, many of them did not occur far out at sea. In fact, one of the reasons why these events are so bizarre is because ships have virtually vanished near the shore—some while sailing in view of a peninsula, for example, or close to a harbor. The same is true of planes—some have disappeared over shallow water and often in the midst of radio contact with a control tower. And in most cases, there is no debris or other clue as to what really happened.

A Variety of Names, a Variety of Shapes

Over the centuries, this area of the Atlantic Ocean has been known by a variety of names—the Hoodoo Sea, the Sea of Oblivion, the Limbo of the Lost, the Sea of Lost Ships, and the Graveyard of the Atlantic, among others. The name that is most commonly used today, however, is the Bermuda Triangle.

Interestingly, experts disagree on its exact perimeter. Some say the area is the triangle formed by connecting the points from Miami, Florida, through the Bahamas to Puerto Rico, and then north to the island of Bermuda. Others say the area is much larger—about 500,000 square miles [804,672 sq km]—and is less triangular than it is rhombus-shaped. This area includes the eastern seaboard of the United States as far north as Wilmington, North Carolina, extends east of Bermuda, and includes the islands of Cuba, Puerto Rico, and Jamaica as well as Haiti and the Dominican Republic in the south.

There are no exact borders or boundaries to the Bermuda Triangle, says oceanographer and Bermuda Triangle expert Martin Caidin. "Even those of us who have flown through the Bermuda Triangle, and sailed it as well, find it necessary at times to alter the sides of 'the Triangle' because of some new event or disturbance that adds another bit of hard data to [it]."[1]

No Official Response

The U.S. military has denied that the Bermuda Triangle is any more mysterious than any other section of the planet's oceans. Military leaders have officially stated that nothing supernatural or strange has occurred there. They insist that what some have called disappearances are accidents that resulted from storms or mechanical failures on planes or boats. They say that while such accidents are tragic, they are simply an unfortunate fact of life, and pilots and seamen understand that such events occur all over the world.

But off the record, many in the military have something different to say. They acknowledge that though the official line is that the Bermuda Triangle is only a myth, those who have flown or sailed in the area know differently. "Nobody in the Navy sneers at this sort of thing," says a U.S. Navy information officer. "We've always known

THE BERMUDA TRIANGLE

Atlantic
Ocean

BERMUDA

BERMUDA
TRIANGLE

Miami

Gulf of
Mexico

BAHAMAS

San
Juan

CUBA

MEXICO

BELIZE

HONDURAS

JAMAICA

HAITI

DOMINICAN
REPUBLIC

PUERTO
RICO

GUATEMALA

EL SALVADOR

NICARAGUA

COSTA RICA

Caribbean Sea

PANAMA

VENEZUELA

There are no exact borders or boundaries to
the Bermuda Triangle, but the most widely
agreed upon perimeter is from Miami,
Florida, through the Bahamas to Puerto
Rico, then north to the island of Bermuda.

COLOMBIA

Source: World Atlas Travel, "Bermuda Triangle," 2008. www.worldatlas.com.

there's something strange about the Bermuda Triangle."[2]

The officer goes on to say that what is especially perplexing about the Bermuda Triangle is that the ships that have disappeared there seem to do so instantly, as if they have simply vanished. "It's almost as if these ships had been suddenly covered by some sort of electronic camouflage net,"[3] he says.

Ideas, but No Answers

As with other mysterious or unexplained phenomena, people have speculated about the reasons for the strange occurrences in the Bermuda Triangle. Some have proposed that unusual magnetic forces under the sea may account for the strange malfunction of instruments and controls, or that the Bermuda Triangle may contain strange currents that could result in megastorms unseen in other places on earth.

Other people have suggested more unusual causes for the disappearances. These ideas have ranged from giant squids to leftover electricity from the lost continent of Atlantis causing the trouble. Several scientists have speculated that UFOs could be responsible, and the victims of the disappearances were actually abducted by those spaceships.

Although no one has yet proven whether the answer is supernatural or scientific in nature, one thing is certain: The fate of more than 1,000 people who have traveled through the Bermuda Triangle remains unknown. As much mystery surrounds the Bermuda Triangle now as 50 years ago. The number of disappearances continues to grow each month. As researcher Gian Quasar notes, in the history of mysteries at sea, "there is no other place that challenges mankind with so many extraordinary and incredible events."[4]

CHAPTER 1

Centuries of Lost Ships

Stories about sailors and ships experiencing trouble within what is now called the Bermuda Triangle have circulated for centuries. In fact, some stories date back to the sixth century B.C., when the Phoenicians, an ancient civilization on the Mediterranean Sea, set out in boats to the west, across the Atlantic Ocean.

They encountered a number of problems in an area that later became known as the Sargasso Sea, a part of the Atlantic that overlaps the eastern part of the Bermuda Triangle. Interestingly, it was not the violent storms or howling winds that frightened these ancient sailors; rather, it was the eerie calm they experienced. There was no wind at all, and with their sails hanging uselessly from the masts, they waited nervously for any breeze that could help them on their way.

The admiral Himilco, from the North African kingdom of Carthage, wrote in 500 B.C. about the odd calmness he and his men encountered when they entered that region—a place where sea monsters lurked:

> No breeze drives the ship, so dead is the sluggish wind of this idle sea. . . . There is much seaweed among the waves, it holds back the ship like bushes. . . . The sea has no great depth, the surface of the earth is barely covered by a little water. . . . The monsters of the sea move continuously to and fro and fierce monsters swim among the sluggish and slowly creeping ships.[5]

No one knows what these monsters might have been. But the stagnant stillness that Himilco and others experienced has a good explanation. As scientists now understand, a number of major

Pictured is the area of the Bermuda Triangle known as the Sargasso Sea, where a number of major ocean currents converge—the North Atlantic Current, the Gulf Stream, and the Equatorial Drift. The water here is very calm and has made many sailors uneasy.

ocean currents converge at the Sargasso Sea—the North Atlantic Current, the Gulf Stream, and the Equatorial Drift. Each comes from a different direction, and as they come together, they revolve in a clockwise direction. This leaves the waters within the Sargasso Sea as smooth as glass and the air cloudless and calm—much like the eye of a violent hurricane.

"It Was like a Small Wax Candle"

Christopher Columbus, during his voyage to the New World in the late fifteenth century, also journeyed through the Sargasso Sea. In his ship's log, he noted the unexplained calm. He also made reference to other odd occurrences, including the apparent malfunction of his navigational compass. Instead of pointing toward the North Star, as it always had, it pointed six degrees to the northwest.

Columbus knew that this would frighten the men in his crew, who were already edgy about this voyage into unknown waters. He kept the compass anomaly to himself to keep his men from panicking. But other odd things occurred as the ship went farther and farther into the Bermuda Triangle. The most confusing was an unexplained light that appeared on October 11, 1492. Columbus himself noticed it and was puzzled. At that point in the voyage they were far from land—too far to see a bonfire or other light from shore.

Another man on the ship, Pero Gutierrez, saw it, too. This "remarkable ball of fire,"[6] as it was later described, was a mystery. "After the Admiral [Columbus used the third person to refer to himself in official records] said it, it was seen once or twice, and it was like a small wax candle that arose and lifted up."[7]

During his voyage to the New World in the late fifteenth century, Christopher Columbus sailed through the Sargasso Sea. In his ship's log, he noted the unexplained calm, the apparent malfunction of his navigational compass, and strange lights.

The Mysteries Continue

No one knows for certain how many other early voyagers encountered problems in the Bermuda Triangle, for almost none of those ships' logs have survived. The modern history of disappearances in the Bermuda Triangle begins in the nineteenth century. Many of

these were merchant vessels, but it is also true that naval ships occasionally vanished, too—even though they were more sturdily constructed than merchant ships and were manned by far more experienced crews.

One of these was the British navy's training ship, HMS *Atalanta*. The *Atalanta* sailed from Bermuda on January 31, 1880, with a crew of 290. By mid-April the British navy announced that the ship was overdue. On April 14, 1880, the London *Times* announced that while the ship was missing, it was too early to assume the worst:

> When the *Atalanta* left Bermuda there were 109 tons [120 U.S. customary tons] of water on board, and an ample supply of provisions. The ship was in all respects sound, possessed of unusual stability, and commanded by an officer of good judgment and high professional qualifications; but the unexpected delay in her arrival affords cause for anxiety for her safety.[8]

But as weeks went by, the ship was believed lost. It was perplexing to experts why then no debris was found from the large ship. While it was never learned exactly where the ship ran into trouble, many believe it occurred in the first 500 miles (805km) of its voyage, when it was going through the heart of the Bermuda Triangle.

Sturdier but Still Vanishing

Over the years ships were made even sturdier and safer. They no longer had to rely on wind and sails and instead had steam engines. They had flares and lifeboats. Even more important, by the early twentieth century, ships had begun using a new invention—wireless radios, which allowed them to communicate with one another or with stations on shore in case of emergency. As one naval historian notes, "Wireless telegraphy [an old term for early radio technology] was to deprive the sea of its ancient terror of silence."[9]

Even with such advances, however, the disappearances in the Bermuda Triangle continued. One of the most baffling of these was that of the USS *Cyclops,* which vanished in 1918, near the end of World War I. The *Cyclops* was a collier, a ship used to transport ore used by industries in the United States that were supplying weapons and other military equipment to the troops. It was very large and heavy—19,000 tons (17,237 metric tons) and 542 feet (165m) long. Only 8 years old, the *Cyclops* was considered one of the U.S. Navy's best ships, with a state-of-the-art radio system.

On its last voyage, it was carrying a crew of 309 men. It was on the last leg of a voyage from Brazil, where it had picked up a load of manganese ore. It had stopped at the Caribbean island of Barbados, and on March 4 it was headed to Norfolk, Virginia. The crew of the *Cyclops* was looking forward to getting back to the United States.

"Only God and the Sea"

However, problems started occurring almost right after the ship left Barbados. Twice it was spotted by British patrol boats nearby, taking turns to the south—the opposite direction from where it was supposed to go. Twice the *Cyclops* was guided back to the correct heading to the north. Soon after it was corrected for the second time, it disappeared.

It was due in Norfolk on March 13, but that day came and went, with no sign of the ship. Navy officials were perplexed. They tracked all weather patterns, and no storms had occurred in the area during that time. They had received no radio distress calls from the *Cyclops*, either. Surely if the ship had experienced any mechanical or other failure it would have sent a message.

Hoping to find the ship drifting off course, the U.S. Navy mounted a massive search with planes and ships, but without success. Not a shred of debris was found, which was highly unusual. The ship seemed to have simply vanished. As President Woodrow Wilson remarked, "Only God and the Sea know where the great ship has gone."[10]

Theories

What had happened to the *Cyclops* caused a great deal of speculation. One theory was that it had been attacked by a German U-boat, or submarine. At first, it seemed a likely theory, for this was indeed wartime. But naval experts were not so sure. The German navy was usually quick to take credit for sinking enemy ships, and it had said nothing about the *Cyclops*.

Another theory was that the huge load of ore may have shifted in the ship's hold, perhaps upsetting the balance of the *Cyclops*. Some even suggested that sudden movement of the ore could have ripped a hole in the bottom of the ship. But with no distress call, and no debris found, experts said that was unlikely, too. The ship was huge, and it was almost impossible to believe that some piece of the ship would not have been discovered by the rescue mission.

One of the most interesting speculations had to do with its captain, George W. Worley. Although he had 28 years of experience and had been in command of the *Cyclops* since its maiden

This German U-Boat was captured by U.S. troops in 1944. When the USS Cyclops disappeared in 1918, some thought a German U-Boat may have sunk it. After the war, an examination of German naval records showed no U-boats had been in the area where the Cyclops had traveled.

"Only God and the sea know where the great ship has gone."

—President Woodrow Wilson, on the strange disappearance of the USS *Cyclops*.

voyage in 1910, he was also of German descent. Some wondered if Worley had been secretly loyal to Germany. They wondered if he had committed an act of treason by turning the ship and its contents over to the German navy. But people who knew Worley well insisted that he would never have betrayed the United States, especially leaving his wife and child behind.

After the war was over, these speculations were proved unfounded. An examination of German naval records showed no U-boats or underwater mines had been in the area where the *Cyclops* had traveled. And no evidence ever proved that Captain Worley had aided the Germans by turning his ship over to the German navy. In a fact sheet issued about the *Cyclops,* the U.S. Navy admits that it is still a riddle that perplexes the experts: "The disappearance of the ship has been one of the most baffling mysteries in the annals of the Navy, all attempts to locate her have proved unsuccessful. . . . Many theories have been advanced, but none that satisfactorily accounts for her disappearance."[11]

The *Carroll A. Deering*

In most of the Bermuda Triangle disappearances, there is no sign of ship or crew. In a few instances, however, ships have been discovered near or within the triangle with no sign of the crew. One of the most famous of these ships was a five-masted schooner called the *Carroll A. Deering.*

The *Deering* was spotted just after dawn on January 31, 1921. A Coast Guard watchman at the Cape Hatteras station in North Carolina was stunned to see a ship that had run aground on nearby Diamond Shoals, a treacherous stretch of shifting sandbars and shallow water that extends miles into the Atlantic Ocean. The weather that morning was blustery and stormy, and it was not until a day later that Coast Guard crews could get close to the *Deering*.

What they saw was astonishing. The ship's records indicated that it carried a crew of 11, but there was no sign of any of them. In fact, the only sign of life was two cats, most likely mascots. It was clear that the humans aboard had left in a hurry, for a meal was in the process of being prepared on the stove. The lifeboats were gone, but the ship seemed to be in surprisingly good shape—structurally and mechanically. But what had become of the crew?

"We Might as Well Have Searched a Painted Ship"

Though the Coast Guard searched for some sign of the crew—dead bodies, lifeboats, and so on—it had no luck. As one federal official said, "We might as well have searched a painted ship on a painted ocean for sight of the vanished."[12]

The mystery fueled a lot of debate about what had happened. Some wondered whether the rough weather had forced the crew members into the lifeboats. But most naval experts refuted that idea. Scientist and former British secret agent Ivan Sanderson, in his book about derelict ships titled *Invisible Residents*, says that for any crew to have left the safety of the large ship for lifeboats would have been very much out of character for all but the most inexperienced seamen: "Certain facts should be noted. First, even an inexperienced or leaderless crew seldom if ever abandon ship because of [a] storm. To do so is obviously asinine, because if the ship won't hold up, no yawl, gig, or other small lifeboat can do so."[13]

Others suggested that perhaps pirates or other criminals could

have been responsible for the missing crew members, but there was no evidence of how that could have happened. What was more perplexing was the report six months later that several other ships had mysteriously disappeared in the same area since the *Deering*'s discovery. Larry Kusche, who is skeptical of the idea of the Bermuda Triangle, admits that the incident is baffling. "The story of the *Carroll A. Deering* is unique in maritime history," he writes, "and it can truly be said that the more that is learned about it, the more mysterious it becomes."[14]

A Mile from Shore

As mysterious as a "ghost ship" with no crew is the disappearance of a ship very close to shore. One of the most intriguing of these was the *Witchcraft*, a cabin cruiser owned by a Miami hotel owner named Dan Burack. The *Witchcraft* disappeared on December 22, 1967, just 1 mile (1.6km) from the Miami shore. Burack had invited a friend, a Catholic priest named Patrick Horgan, out on his boat. They were going to relax by taking the boat 1 mile (1.6km) out and enjoy the Christmas lights that were visible along the shore.

At 9:00 P.M. Burack sent a radio distress call to the Coast Guard. He said that his propeller had struck something underwater and that his engine could not run very well. He needed a tow in, but he assured the Coast Guard that he was in no danger. He specifically gave his location as the Number 7 lifebuoy, right at the entrance to Miami's harbor. The Coast Guard dispatcher requested that Burack send up a flare in about 20 minutes, so the boat easily could be seen.

Within a few minutes a boat was on its way, and 19 minutes after the distress call was sent, the Coast Guard had arrived at

The Horse Latitudes

In the days when oceangoing ships depended on wind for their sails, there was a particular area of the Atlantic Ocean (included within the Sargasso Sea) that was greatly feared. Known as the "horse latitudes," it was notorious for its lack of wind. Ships could be stranded for days or even weeks there, and supplies of food and water would run out.

Its name had a gruesome origin. When the first Spanish explorers and traders journeyed to the New World, they brought horses with them. Horses require a great deal of water to drink, but when the ships became stuck in a certain part of the Sargasso Sea, there was often not enough drinking water for both humans and horses. The sailors were forced to kill the horses and throw them overboard. Other ships passing through the area frequently saw the remains of the horses—hence the term *horse latitudes*. The sight only increased the sailors' fears of an already eerie place.

the Number 7 lifebuoy. However, there was absolutely no sign of the *Witchcraft.* It was as if it had never been there at all.

No Cause for Alarm

Interestingly, however, the Coast Guard was not overly concerned at first. The boat could not have been swept away from the lifebuoy in 19 minutes. The boat was missing, but experts believed that it was very unlikely that Burack and Horgan were in any real trouble. Even those who knew the two men well were confident that they would turn up unharmed. "Dan's an expert sailor and a good navigator," said one. "I don't know if Father Horgan can swim, but Dan can, and neither of them is the type to panic in an emergency. . . . They were carrying all the safety devices on the boat, too."[15]

It was well known, too, that the *Witchcraft* had been well equipped in case of unforeseen trouble. Burack was known to be extremely safety conscious, and besides stocking the *Witchcraft* with numerous life preservers and floating seat cushions, he had spent a great deal of money adding extra built-in flotation to the boat's hull. That meant that even if the boat had been struck by another boat, there would have been some evidence on the surface. "Although this [added flotation to the hull] does not imply buoyancy," explains expert Gian Quasar, "it does mean that some part of the vessel, even when waterlogged, should remain visible above the water."[16]

The circumstances seemed very odd. Burack had given a specific location—he was not lost at sea. He had radioed the Coast Guard, so his boat had power. But then why had he not turned his own lights on, and why had he not sent up the requested flare? A massive search was later launched, covering more than 1,200 square miles (3,108 sq. km) of ocean. But no sign of the men or the boat was ever found.

No Clues

Such strange and unexplained disappearances have continued through the years. Of course, ships and smaller boats disappear everywhere. Storms occur, and people make foolish mistakes that can lead to the sinking of their boats. But nowhere on the planet do more disappear than in the Bermuda Triangle.

More importantly, except for a handful of "ghost ships" whose crews vanished, such as the *Carroll A. Deering*, the ships and boats lost within the triangle actually disappear, meaning that their remains are never found. That, say experts, is astonishingly unlikely. The ocean, especially in the southern part of the triangle (where most of the disappearances occur) is not as deep as it is in most places. The wrecks of ships that have gone down in storms or have sunk because of accidents or wartime attacks are evident there—some even visible from the surface of the water.

But the Bermuda Triangle's more mysterious victims are another story. Even though there have been many attempts to find evidence of these vessels on the ocean floor, none has been successful. Instead, notes triangle researcher Quasar, it appears that these unlucky ships and boats "sailed away silently without one word or clear SOS [distress signal], even without their automatic alarms to indicate they sank."[17]

CHAPTER 2

Vanishing from the Air

While scores of documents record missing ships and boats within the Bermuda Triangle, it was not until airplanes began to disappear within that area that its mysterious reputation began to solidify. For one reason, planes are far more unlikely than ships to simply disappear. They are in almost constant radio contact with those on the ground, and they can check in immediately if they have mechanical issues or are experiencing bad weather. Finally, because they usually take off and land within a few hours' time, they are rarely out of range of a control tower's radar screen.

Even so, planes have nonetheless been disappearing regularly within the Bermuda Triangle—from small private planes to military bombers and passenger jets. Many have disappeared right off a radar screen as they have been coming in for a landing. In

An air traffic controller monitors flights in the control tower at Newark International Airport in New Jersey. Planes are far more unlikely than ships to simply disappear. They are in almost constant radio contact with air traffic control, and they can check in immediately if they have mechanical issues or are experiencing bad weather. They are also rarely out of range of a control tower's radar screen.

more than a few cases, they have vanished in the midst of talking to an air traffic controller.

The most famous of all these disappearances occurred in 1945, when five U.S. Navy bombers and a plane dispatched to investigate their sudden disappearance vanished during a training exercise. According to Bermuda Triangle expert Charles Berlitz, "No incident before or since has been more remarkable than this *total* disappearance of an entire training flight, along with the giant rescue plane, a Martin Mariner with a crew of thirteen, which inexplicably vanished during rescue operations."[18]

Flight 19

The crews taking off that day on December 5, 1945, were not concerned about enemy engagement in the air. The war had ended 4 months earlier. Flight 19, as this group of bombers was known that day, was actually a training mission. The men were going to practice their bombing techniques first on a wrecked target ship off the coast of Bimini, an island about 52 miles (84km) east of Miami. After that, they were going to fly east over the ocean to work on advanced navigational skills over the open water.

The 5 planes were TBM-3 Avenger bombers, the largest single-engine planes used by the U.S. military during World War II. Each of them had enough fuel to last for 1,000 miles (1,609km) of flying, or approximately 5.5 hours of flight—although the entire exercise was estimated to take only about 2 hours.

Fourteen men were aboard—one man short that day—and all were experienced. The officer in command was Lieutenant Charles Taylor, a 6-year veteran pilot with more than 2,500 hours of flying time. The other 4 pilots were all accomplished as well, each with at least 350 flight hours.

"Everything Is Wrong"

As Flight 19 took off at 2:00 P.M., it promised to be a relatively routine flight. The weather was clear and mild—perfect for flying. After doing their bombing practice over Bimini, Taylor and his squadron headed farther east, as planned. But then, unexpectedly, a problem occurred.

Taylor radioed one of the other pilots, Charles Powers, and told him that his compasses were acting strangely. They seemed erratic, and as a result, he was unsure of his direction. The other pilots began comparing their own readings, but they could not agree. Two of the pilots were certain that they needed to head west, but the other three were not sure. At 3:15 P.M., the controllers at Fort Lauderdale Air Force Base received a distress signal from Taylor:

> Calling Tower. This is an emergency. We seem to be off course. We cannot see land. . . . Repeat. . . . We cannot see land. . . . [When controllers asked for his position, he replied:] We are not sure of our position. We cannot be sure just where we are. . . . We seem to be lost. . . . [When told to head west, Taylor replied,] We don't know which way is west. Everything is wrong. . . . Strange. . . . We can't be sure of any direction—even the ocean doesn't look as it should.[19]

Did You Know?

Flight 19 vanished four months after the end of World War II.

"Don't Come After Me"

At this same time, another flight instructor, Lieutenant Robert Cox, was flying in the vicinity and heard the radio messages between Taylor and the other pilots as they argued about their compasses. He asked what was wrong, and when they told him they were unsure of where they were going, he offered assistance on how to return to Fort Lauderdale. "Put the sun on your port [left] wing if you are in the Keys," he advised, "and fly up the coast until you get to Miami, then Fort Lauderdale is twenty miles further, your first port after Miami. The air station is directly on your left from the port."[20]

Cox then asked what their present altitude was, and he offered to meet them so he could guide them to the air base. But instead of accepting the help, Taylor refused. "I'm at 2,300 feet (701m)," he told Cox. "Don't come after me."[21] Disregarding

Taylor's request that he not come after the squadron, Cox headed to where Taylor said he was. But no one was there. That seemed very strange, especially as his radio reception with Flight 19 was getting worse, not better. Clearly, he was getting farther from Taylor and his squadron.

The air control tower had begun losing radio contact with Flight 19, too. In an effort to maintain communication, the controller requested that Taylor switch to a different frequency. But Taylor refused, saying that he worried that if he did so, he might lose contact with the other four planes in his squadron.

So as the reception faded, the control tower was unable to do anything but listen to static-filled bits of conversation between the pilots. They heard them say their compasses were "going crazy."[22] They heard arguing among the men, and finally, they heard nothing at all.

Missing Five, Missing Six

The control tower at Fort Lauderdale air base wasted no time in sending help. It sent up a Martin Mariner, a huge boat patrol plane, to search for the missing planes. The Mariner, with a crew of 13 men, sent a radio message soon after takeoff, but within 20 minutes it, too, had disappeared. No radio message, no SOS, no signal

indicated that it was experiencing difficulty. It seemed that the tally of vanished planes was now 6, the toll of missing men now 27.

A massive search began the next morning at dawn, but no sign of the 6 planes could be found. This was very puzzling to authorities, who insisted that some debris would be left if 6 planes had crashed. For one thing, there would there have been oil slicks on the surface of the water. And the Avengers were all equipped with self-inflating rafts. Even if the men had been killed or otherwise unable to use them, they would have floated on the surface to be visible to the search teams. But there seemed no explanation for the mass disappearance. Though the navy's Board of Review studied the incident thoroughly, it came up with no answers. As one member of the Board of Review commented with frustration, "They vanished as completely as if they had flown to Mars."[23]

The *Star Tiger*

Although Flight 19 remains the strangest case of air disappearances within the Bermuda Triangle, it is certainly not the only one that has puzzled authorities. Early on the morning of January 30, 1948, the British luxury airliner the *Star Tiger* and its 32 passengers vanished mysteriously in the Bermuda Triangle.

This Avenger aircraft is the same kind of plane that was lost in the Bermuda Triangle in 1945. It is also the same type that was found off the coast of Fort Lauderdale in 1991 by the crew of the Deep See.

During the Flight 19
tragedy, a total of
27 crew members
(from six planes)
disappeared.

The *Star Tiger* was on the last leg of its journey from London. It had stopped in the Azores, islands west of Portugal, before beginning the almost 2,000 mile (3,219km) trip to Hamilton, Bermuda. The sky was clear as the *Star Tiger* took off on the night of January 29. Just after 1:00 A.M. the pilot sent a radio message, saying that the ship was 440 miles (708km) northeast of Bermuda and everything was going smoothly. But when the *Star Tiger* was overdue in Bermuda, controllers there became concerned, and their concern grew as they tried without success to communicate with the plane.

However, authorities on the ground did not panic. They knew, for example, that the captain and crew were very experienced. They knew that the plane could float, and they hoped that if there had been some emergency, the pilot could have ditched, or made an emergency landing on the water. If the pilot ditched, the design of the plane gave passengers a good chance of survival. Notes researcher John Wallace Spencer, "The [plane] is sufficiently pressurized and . . . sealed that, if undamaged, would allow everyone aboard to get set free in the rubber life rafts she carried."[24] In addition, each life raft carried a crank-style radio that would enable them to communicate SOS messages that could be picked up by planes and ships within 100 miles (161km) or so of their position.

No Sign

Air-sea search teams began looking for the plane. More than 40 airplanes and numerous Coast Guard vessels took part in the search. Based on the *Star Tiger*'s last radio communication at 1:00 A.M., search teams had the plane's precise location, and they headed immediately to the area between that point and the Bermuda coast. But after covering more than 200,000 square miles (517,998 sq. km) of ocean, the search teams were baffled. There was no sign of the plane, any lifeboats, or even an oil slick—something that would have been on the surface if the plane had crashed.

The authorities were genuinely perplexed. The disappearance made absolutely no sense. There had not been an emergency distress call, which any experienced pilot would have made. Perhaps the crisis was so instantaneous that there had been no time. But with perfect flying weather, what could that crisis have been? With each passing hour, hope and optimism turned to dismay.

An eerie development occurred on February 3, four days after the *Star Tiger* had gone missing. A naval station in Newfoundland, Canada, reported that it had received a verbal message—someone's voice saying only the letters GAHNP, which were the call letters of the missing plane. Likewise, radio operators up and down the Atlantic coast, from Miami to Canada, began reporting coded messages spelling out T-I-G-E-R. Unfortunately, it is not uncommon for some people to take advantage of such tragedies by supplying false information, and some authorities denounced the anonymous messages as hoaxes. But others were not so sure. So much about the *Star Tiger*'s disappearance was strange, it was hard to know what to believe, and what could be discounted.

"An Unsolved Mystery" Times Two

Britain's Civil Air Ministry conducted a thorough eight-month-long investigation of the *Star Tiger*'s disappearance, but it found nothing that could explain it. The report was interesting, however, because of what it eliminated as causes for the tragedy—ruling out pilot error, weather, and even structural problems with the plane.

The Civil Air Ministry's report admitted that investigators had no idea at all what had occurred, saying only that it was an occurrence that would likely never be explained:

Torpedo Bomber #28 (pictured) was the lead plane from the lost squadron that vanished in 1945. The crew pictured, however, is not the crew that vanished with Flight 19. The planes that flew in that mission have also never been recovered.

Did You Know?

Lieutenant Charles Taylor of Flight 19 had more than 2,500 hours of flying time.

In closing this report, it may truly be said that no more baffling problem has ever been presented for investigation. In the complete absence of any reliable evidence as to the nature or the cause of the accident to *Star Tiger* the court has not been able to do more than to suggest possibilities, none of which reaches the level of probability. . . . What happened in this case will never be known and the fate of *Star Tiger* must remain an unsolved mystery.[25]

The "unsolved mystery" became even more bizarre when the *Star Tiger*'s sister aircraft, the *Star Ariel*, disappeared less than a year later under similar circumstances. On January 17, 1949, after stopping to refuel in Bermuda, it took off in calm, clear weather. An hour after takeoff, the pilot reported that everything was fine. That, however, was the *Star Ariel*'s last communication. A massive search was launched with 72 planes; at times, says researcher Charles Berlitz, the planes were flying "wing tip to wing tip"[26] over 150,000 square miles (388,498 sq. km) of ocean. But again, as with the other disappearances in the triangle, there was no sign of the plane or its passengers and crew.

The Flying Boxcar

The disappearance of a U.S. Air Force aircraft in 1965 added a mysterious new twist to the growing legend of the Bermuda Triangle. This type of plane was a C-119, a huge twin-tailed aircraft that was nicknamed "the Flying Boxcar" because it had an oversized cargo area. In fact, the C-119 was so big and bulky that crews used to joke that it "traveled so slowly that the earth rotated beneath it."[27]

On June 5, 1965, the plane had 10 passengers—a maintenance

crew from Milwaukee's 440th Airlift Wing. The journey was a quick one—to drop off an airplane engine and crew on Grand Turk Island in the Bahamas. The flight seemed routine—the plane took off on time in clear, calm weather. The captain sent a standard radio message that all was fine, and he gave his position as being about 100 miles (161km) from his destination. But when time went on without any sign of the plane, radio operators in New York, Miami, Puerto Rico, and Grand Turk Island all tried to communicate with the C-119 without success. There was only silence.

Experts, including fellow members of the 440th, were confused by the circumstances. The crew was highly experienced, and the passengers were all trained mechanics. Surely if there had been some mechanical trouble with the plane, they could have found a way to fix it. Besides, they were all capable of finding a way to either make an emergency landing or, if nothing else, radio a message to the ground. And if they had had to ditch, there were lots of bright yellow life rafts that had been packed on the plane that would have enabled the men to stay afloat until help arrived.

Friends and fellow members of the 440th wondered if there had been something instantaneous that had happened. "It has to be an explosion or something for them not to say anything," said Osbee Sampson, a maintenance crew member from the 440th who saw the C-119 take off that day. "Even if you're having trouble, you switch on the radio so they can track you. There had to have been a big bang."[28]

But if an explosion had occurred, why had no debris been found? No ships in the area had reported hearing a loud bang, and another C-119 flying the same route in the other direction at the same time saw and heard nothing unusual. The U.S. Air Force was stymied, and it seemed that there was no explanation that made any sense.

From Tragedy to Enigma

Bermuda Triangle researcher Gian Quasar believes that Flight 19 was the key force behind the triangle's reputation for mysterious occurrences. In his book *Into the Bermuda Triangle: Pursuing the Truth Behind the World's Greatest Mystery*, Quasar writes, "There seems to be no logical explanation for the disappearance of five aircraft, or for the many confusing reports that night [December 5, 1945]. . . . Blaming any pilot cannot

A UFO and the Flying Boxcar?

But there was an interesting sidebar to the disappearance of the Flying Boxcar—an eyewitness account of an unidentified flying object (UFO) in the area at the time the plane vanished. And while reports of UFOs are often quickly dismissed by authorities, this report came from a very reputable source—an American astronaut.

James McDivitt and Ed White were high above the earth in their *Gemini 4* space capsule. At the same time the Flying Boxcar was approaching Grand Turk Island in the Bahamas, McDivitt

explain the lack of debris or bodies at sea. When pondering all of these, it is not surprising that the enigma of the Bermuda Triangle developed and in turn maintained a tight grip over the incident. An entire fleet of 5 planes plus one rescue plane—carrying a combined total of 27 men—completely vanished.

"If this had been an isolated incident, it would remain a great mystery of aviation. However, continuing disappearances of aircraft afterward, many in the same area, and some with drawn-out and confusing radio messages like Flight 19's, indicate that perhaps it is only one of many, all sharing a similar cause or at least some crucial factor before meeting the same fate."

observed a strange flying object that seemed to be hovering over the Caribbean Sea—something he had never seen before. He later described what happened:

> It had a very definite shape, a white cylindrical object. It had a long arm that stuck out on the side. We had two cameras that were floating around [in the capsule], so I grabbed one and took a picture. Then I turned on the rocket control systems because I was

afraid we might hit it. I called down later and told [mission control] what had happened. They went back and checked their records but were never able to identify what it could have been.[29]

Ed White was able to confirm McDivitt's observation, but neither man had any idea what they were seeing. But their observation led some to speculate on a new explanation for the disappearances in the triangle. Was there some sort of UFO connection to the planes and boats that had vanished over the years?

Roger Johnson is an amateur pilot who has flown hundreds of times within the Bermuda Triangle, "It sounded kind of goofy to start talking about UFOs interfering with pilots traveling through the Bermuda Triangle. But I guess when McDivitt, a NASA astronaut, sees something that can't be identified—in the same area as the plane was when it disappeared, it doesn't sound quite so goofy."[30]

Still Happening

Reports of planes gone missing in the Bermuda Triangle have continued into the twenty-first century. For example, in 2002 a small Cessna plane vanished as the pilot was talking to a Miami control tower. Though the pilot was only a few miles from the landing strip at the time, no trace of the plane was found. In 2007 a Piper plane disappeared as it was coming in for a landing in the Bahamas. The plane was on the radar screen, controllers maintained, and all of a sudden—it was not.

Such stories have helped to solidify the Bermuda Triangle's reputation as a dangerous and mysterious place. But interest-

This is an illustration of a C-119 plane. The C-119 was nicknamed the "Flying Boxcar" because of its huge cargo area. On June 5, 1965 a C-119 with 10 crew members aboard went missing in the Triangle.

ingly, the mystery has been strengthened even more by the ships and planes that do not vanish, but whose crews experience close calls while in the area. They live to tell about what they saw and heard, and in many cases, their stories continue to make their listeners' blood run cold.

CHAPTER 3

Near Misses in the Triangle

Those who have lived through danger or weird occurrences within the Bermuda Triangle range from commercial airline crews to air force and navy personnel, from amateur sailors and pilots to men and women with decades of flying and sailing experience. Many are unwilling to share their Triangle experiences with others for fear of being ridiculed. "Things like [I experienced] have happened to other pilots," says professional pilot Chuck Wakely, "but they don't like to talk about it."[31]

Florida sailor Brian Hennessy agrees. He has two good friends who have experienced odd things in the area but would never report them:

> These guys have had equipment malfunctions, compasses not working all of a sudden, stuff like

that. And they would never report it, except for telling a few trusted friends. It's like a lot of people who have seen a UFO—and I don't mean a space ship. I'd venture to guess that a lot of us who spend time at sea have seen things in the night sky that we can't identify. I'll tell my wife, my sons, a couple of friends. But that's not the same thing as going public. You just don't want to get a reputation for being nuts. And there will be some who will think that, unfortunately.[32]

But luckily for Bermuda Triangle researchers, some people have survived in odd, scary situations. Their stories have given researchers some ideas about what might have caused the disappearances of thousands of people within the Bermuda Triangle. Perhaps the missing victims of the triangle had experienced the same problems or odd circumstances, but unlike the survivors, they were unable to regain their bearings so that they could return alive to tell about it.

Glowing Wings

A number of pilots have experienced what appear to be electrical oddities when over the Bermuda Triangle. Chuck Wakely recalls flying between Miami and Nassau in November 1964. The weather was clear, and the sky was filled with stars. Wakely was more than familiar with the area and its weather patterns, and he says that up until that night, there was nothing that he had not seen. But that changed as he headed back to Miami on the return trip.

"I began to notice something unusual—a very faint glowing effect on the wings," he told researcher Charles Berlitz. "At first I

thought it was an illusion created by the cockpit lights shining through the tinted Plexiglas windows, because the wings had a translucent appearance, appearing pale blue-green, although they were actually painted bright-white."[33]

As Wakely kept an eye on the plane's wings, he saw that the glow increased, becoming brighter and brighter. At the same time, his cockpit instruments began acting strangely, too. For instance, the fuel gauge that had just minutes before read as half full now indicated a full tank. Wakely had been using autopilot (much like cruise control in an automobile), but all of a sudden that caused his plane to veer in a hard right turn.

At that point, he says, the glow became so bright that the whole aircraft radiated light. "The glow was so intense that I could no longer see the stars,"[34] he reported. Unable to control the movements of the plane, he simply let go, allowing the aircraft to fly without resistance. Gradually, Wakely says, the glow began to fade and the instruments soon began to work again—although he has never been able to explain what occurred.

Static on the Windshield

In 1973 reporter Robert Durant interviewed a pilot who had also experienced what appeared to be an unusual glow on his plane. The pilot, who had requested anonymity, told Durant that he was flying from New York to San Juan, Puerto Rico, and that he was expecting very choppy skies on that flight. Pilots flying on that route are used to the turbulence, he explained. They usually tell passengers to keep their seat belts on throughout the flight since unsecured passengers have on occasion found themselves being hurled around the cabin by the turbulence.

But on this particular flight, the skies were calm. The pilot recalled that the crew had been pleasantly surprised and had commented on how smooth the flight was. However, almost immediately after that, streaks of vivid purple static electricity began forming on the plane's windshield. It grew brighter and brighter until a glaring white glow coated the glass. The lack of turbulence proved it could not have been an electrical storm. Neither the pilot nor any of the crew had the slightest explanation for what was happening.

Within a few minutes, the instruments in the cockpit began acting strangely, too. Compasses and other dials on the pilot's side gave different readings than those on the copilot's side. And as had happened to Chuck Wakely years before, the autopilot caused the plane to veer off course.

Without being able to trust his instruments, the pilot took out a portable gyroscope that was kept on board in case of emergencies when the instrument panel did not work. Using that gyroscope, he was able to regain his bearings and make an emergency landing in Bermuda. The pilot said that he never had any explanation for the odd static electricity on the plane's windshield that seemed to cause the malfunctions.

"A Giant Hand"

Many pilots have reported unusual blasts of turbulence as they have flown through the Bermuda Triangle. These blasts seem to come out of nowhere—without any warning signs of storms or high winds. One such case occurred in 1952 and was reported by Gerald Hawkes, a passenger on a commercial flight between New York City and Bermuda.

As the plane got close to its island destination, it suddenly dropped about 200 feet (61m) straight down. Yet it did not feel

The sophisticated flight instruments in a cockpit (pictured) have at times reportedly lost their use while the plane is in the Bermuda Triangle. Pilots report such problems as spinning compasses, sudden unexplained drops in altitude, inability to control steering, trouble with radio communication, and lack of temperature control in the cabin.

like a nose dive, Hawkes later insisted to an interviewer. Rather, he compared the feeling to suddenly falling down an elevator shaft in the air and then, just as suddenly, shooting upward again. Hawkes said, "It was as if a giant hand was holding the plane and jerking it up and down."[35] Hawkes also described the wings of the plane flapping like the wings of a bird.

There seemed no reasonable explanation. The weather was clear, and there were no fierce winds or squalls. Even so, the battering of the plane went on for more than a half hour, with the passengers and crew fearing for their lives. But when the battering finally stopped, there was another problem—the captain had no idea where they were. He was unable to get a radio signal from either the United States or Bermuda. Eventually, however, he contacted a radio ship in the area, which assisted him in finding his way to the Bermuda airport.

A Whirlwind from Nowhere

More than 40 years later, John Macone, who has worked for many years as a professional stunt, or aerobatic, pilot, had a similarly frightening experience as he was landing his small Cessna plane at the Culebra, Puerto Rico, airport. As he made his approach to the airport, there were only light winds—between 6 and 8 knots. However, as the plane began to land, 2 huge blasts of air from the right side jolted the plane.

Macone was able to regain control, but a sudden third blast of air picked up the plane and tossed it as if it were a toy. The jolt, reports researcher Gian Quasar, "threw it 60 to 80 feet [18 to 24m] to the left over buildings, over tension wires, across a road, and then slammed it down into an alleyway, despite any defensive action Macone tried."[36]

Macone and his passenger were hurt, but they survived the incident—due largely to his experience as an aerobatic pilot. However, more than 14 years later the experience still baffles Macone. "In thousands of hours of mountain and aerobatic flying," he says, "I have never encountered a condition approaching the severity of this whirlwind, nor the sense of helplessness it created."[37]

"I Fell Back to the Floor on My Knees"

Such forceful jolts affect larger modern planes, too. On July 8, 1999, a Continental Airlines jet with 155 passengers aboard was flying south of Bermuda, en route to Puerto Rico. The plane unexpectedly suffered massive jolts that caused it to drop crazily more than 600 feet (183m) before the crew could recover.

Leslie Thomas, a flight attendant on that airliner, later recalled the tremendous force and its physical effect on her:

> The crew had just completed the meal service and I was in the back in the aft of the main cabin, approximately row 29, picking up trays from a meal service. The seat belt sign was off and we were flying in smooth air with no sign of turbulence. Then all of a sudden, the aircraft dropped abruptly which caused my body to fly upward hitting my head on the ceiling. I fell back to the floor on my knees. Approximately 10 seconds later, the aircraft dropped again, causing my head to hit the ceiling once again. At that point I lost consciousness. When I awoke, I was very dazed noticing my head bleeding, arms cut and bruised, and back and shoulders sore.[38]

The captain of the plane, Joe Moore, is adamant that the jolts were entirely unexpected. He says that there was nothing at all on the radar or any of his other instruments that indicated the presence of turbulence. "No reports . . . were reported by the ATC [air traffic control], along our route of flight or in our dispatched paperwork. . . . It had been smooth. . . . There were no visual clues to an adverse ride."[39]

But with the crew shaken and 71 of the passengers hurt, that turbulence had been very real. And for researchers and others interested in the unusual goings-on in the triangle, the incident raised an interesting idea: If even professional, experienced pilots encountered such near misses with these unexpected jolts, it seemed logical that less experienced pilots in the same circumstances might have been easily overwhelmed—and could have vanished without a trace.

Ready for Anything

Some survivors in the Bermuda Triangle say their ordeals were marked by a bizarre discrepancy between where they were going and where they actually ended up. Andy Raymond, a scientist from Chicago, lived in the triangle area from 1979 to 1982 while researching solar power and working on an accelerated wind lab. He lived on a small island in the Bahamas, but he often commuted to other islands while he was there.

Raymond says that up until his adventure on July 5, 1980, the only odd thing that he had noticed on some of these short trips was that once in a while the magnetic compass in the airplane would spin "as though powered by an electric motor."[40] Raymond is a scientist, however, and though he knew that there were stories of strange things that had occurred in the Bermuda Triangle, he dismissed most of them as superstition or just bad luck.

But something happened on that day in 1980 that would change his mind. He left his island that day with a friend, Howard Smith—an excellent pilot. The two stopped in Grand Harbor for lunch and then took off again, heading north to Little Stirrup Cay, just an hour's flight away. It was a sunny, clear day, and

Raymond recalls noticing how smooth and glassy the sea appeared as he looked down from the plane. That would change in a hurry.

Soon after their plane took off, heading north, thick clouds began to appear. Neither man was concerned, however. The plane was well equipped with a DME (distance measuring equipment, a device that measures the relationship of time and distance traveled during flight), a great radio, and both electric and magnetic compasses. Smith and Raymond were "flying blind"—an aviation term that meant the weather was so foul that they relied exclusively on their instruments to navigate—but everything was under control.

Copper-Colored Water

Within a short time the plane's DME alerted Smith that they had reached their destination. He dropped back down below the clouds, intending to make his preparations for landing. But as the plane dropped lower, the men realized that there was no Little Stirrup Cay in sight. In fact, all they could see was the ocean below, and it looked unlike any ocean they had ever seen before. "It looked just like boiling copper," Raymond recalled later. "I have seen every kind of light effect the sun can bounce off the surface, but never anything remotely approaching this."[41]

Smith quickly decided to radio the Fort Lauderdale control tower for help, but he discovered that the radio was dead. Descending a bit more, the plane suddenly plummeted 500 feet (152m) in what they assumed was a strong downdraft. That happened several more times, until they finally descended below the clouds.

All of a sudden, the ocean was blue and the skies clear. However, Raymond and Smith were flabbergasted to see that instead of being at Little Stirrup Cay, they were back at Grand Harbor.

WHAT CAUSES THE STRANGE ACTIVITY?

This poll shows that about 20 percent of respondents believe that electromagnetic fields have something to do with the strange activity in the Bermuda Triangle. The majority, 57 percent, think that natural phenomena are the cause of the disappearance of planes and ships.

Question: What causes the disappearance of ships and planes in the Bermuda Triangle?

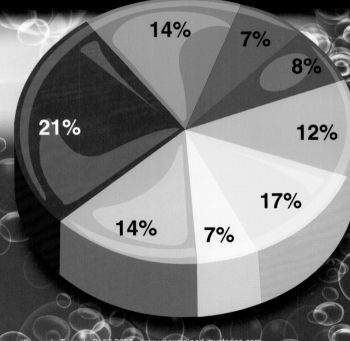

14%

7%

8%

12%

21%

17%

14%

7%

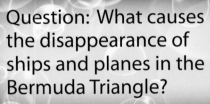

- electromagnetic fields
- storms
- gases from ocean floor
- Atlantis
- aliens
- wormholes
- a mixture of things
- I don't think there is anything strange

Source: Unexplained-mysteries.com, "Bermuda Triangle Poll," 2008. www.unexplained-mysteries.com.

A DME is an instrument that measures the relation of time and distance traveled during an airplane flight.

They had flown in a straight line in the opposite direction but had ended up exactly where they had started. To this day, the men have been unable to come up with an explanation.

"A Big Caulifower"

Whereas Andy Raymond had noticed a copper-colored ocean during his frightening adventure, the crew of one Boeing 707 was more concerned with the odd shape of the water beneath them. They were flying from San Juan, Puerto Rico, to New York on April 11, 1963. At the time of the unusual occurrence, they were in the Bermuda Triangle over what is called the Puerto Rico Trench. This is one of the deepest underwater canyons in the Atlantic Ocean, descending 5.5 miles (9km) below the water's surface.

Twenty minutes after takeoff, as the jet was flying at about 31,000 feet (9449m), the copilot saw something that caused him to do a double take. The ocean below, to the starboard (right) side, was rising in a great round shape that looked like an atomic explosion had occurred below the surface. The copilot, who later described the shape of the water as "a big cauliflower,"[42] quickly pointed it out to the captain and the flight engineer, and they all clambered to the starboard windows to look at it.

The crew estimated the "cauliflower" to be between .5 and 1 mile (.8 and 1.6km) wide and half as tall. Though they were fascinated at the sight, they were reluctant to get closer, in case it was dangerous. When they finally landed in New York, the pilot called the Coast Guard as well as the Federal Bureau of Investigation, but no one knew anything about a natural or man-made event that would cause such a thing. One thing seemed certain: Any ship that had been unlucky enough to be in the area of that water formation would have disappeared instantly.

A State-of-the-Art Catalina

Many harrowing triangle ordeals involve the malfunction of instruments—compasses, gyroscopes, radios, and so on. One of the oddest of these experiences happened to Martin Caidin, a highly experienced pilot who has flown dozens of types of planes in and through the Bermuda Triangle, from charter planes to military aircraft. Caidin prefaces his story by insisting that he believes that the triangle is usually no more dangerous than any other place on earth. Hundreds of thousands of flights through it, he says, occur "without even the cough of an engine or the unexplained twitch of an instrument dial."[43]

That said, however, he also notes that he will never forget what happened on June 11, 1986. Caidin and his wife, Dee Dee (also a pilot), were with friends on their last leg of a long journey that had taken them from Texas to Canada, through the Azores, into Portugal and Spain, into southern England, and then back to Bermuda. They were in a "flying boat," a large plane called a Consolidated PBY-6A Catalina. The other passengers were also experienced pilots, a handful of veteran U.S. Air Force and Navy pilots and airplane mechanics. They were, says Caidin, "veteran, experienced, skilled, ability-recognized . . . who'd flown through, over, and around most of the world."[44]

Caidin also says that the Catalina had been refurbished with state-of-the-art technology rarely found in a private plane. The owners had invested millions of dollars in electronics and equipment—2 of everything, just in case something failed. There was a device that could measure the height of the waves below down to the accuracy of 12 inches (30cm). There was an amazing weather communications system, too. "We wanted to know what the weather was like, we didn't even have to look outside, we were getting direct printout

Bad News for the *Good News*

Former U.S. Navy seaman Don Henry worked as an underwater salvage operator in the Caribbean and along the eastern coast of the United States. He says that the only thing that ever occurred for which he had no explanation was when he was on his boat, the *Good News*, towing a barge through the Bermuda Triangle. First, the instruments on his boat all failed, which had never happened before. That was followed by something even stranger: When he looked behind the *Good News*, he could no longer see the barge!

photos on maps from satellites more than 20,000 miles [32,187km] above."[45] Their navigational equipment was amazing, too—letting them know whether they were even .10 mile (.16km) off course.

"There was no barge," Henry says in an online article posted at the Web site Bermuda-Triangle.org. "We had felt no snap. . . . The towline was leading back the way it was supposed to be, but there was simply no barge. . . . I've likened it to the old Indian rope trick. The towline was just sticking out of a fog . . . but the fog was nowhere else. It was just around where the barge should be. . . . We plowed ahead, or tried to. It seemed that something was pulling us back. It was like being in the middle of two people pulling on your arms."

Eventually, Henry and his crew were able to drag themselves from the area, and the barge reappeared—much warmer than it would have normally been. And there was no sign or explanation for the odd fog that appeared where the barge should have been.

"In the Middle of a Bottle of Eggnog"

As the Catalina headed toward Bermuda on that beautiful June morning, Caidin looked out the window and was surprised. It

seemed that the left wing of the plane had disappeared. Had they flown into a huge cloud or a bank of fog? He checked the weather communications system, but the photos showed nothing. In fact, the closest clouds were more than 200 miles (322km) away.

He moved to the starboard side of the plane and saw that the right wing was no longer visible. And, as they all realized, the cockpit windows showed that it was impossible to see anything up ahead of them. The sky, Caidin says, had turned instantly from blue to a creamy yellow, "as though we were in a bottle of eggnog."[46]

More alarming was the instrument panel. It seemed to have gone completely crazy, with dials swinging back and forth, then rapidly whirling in circles. There was no hint of why they all had failed, nor of why the blue sky had turned suddenly to this strange, murky yellow. Pilots depend on their instruments for speed, altitude, navigation—everything. But there was nothing that worked, and that was frightening. "We had a zillion bucks worth of super electronics in this airplane," Caidin says, "and abruptly they began to fall over as if paralyzed."[47]

No Answers

Caidin says that they all stayed calm, realizing there was nothing they could do. They were over water, so landing was impossible. And with zero visibility in the yellowish soup that had enveloped them, they just tried to stay on what they hoped was the right course.

After about 90 minutes, they flew out of that soup. The sky was crystal clear, and the instruments all came back online. They swung the plane around to get a look at whatever it was that they had been stuck in, but there was no sign of anything. They landed at their destination with no trouble at all.

Caidin says that any scientist will insist that what happened to them that day was impossible. The sky just does not become yellowish soup, causing instruments to die. And such a soup would not just disappear—he and his companions should have been able to see it once they swung around after getting back into the clear.

Caidin believes that somehow the Catalina had found itself enveloped by an intense electromagnetic field that affected the instruments. Though he is unsure of what exactly caused it, he is almost certain that the Catalina had experienced a near miss, barely avoiding one of the eerie phenomena that may have caused the crashes and disappearances of other travelers in the Bermuda Triangle:

> Where did [the electromagnetic field] come from? No one knows. Or was it really an electromagnetic field? No one knows that either. But the point was made that any pilot caught in that "soup" who lacked the experienced flying skills with basic instruments and no outside reference would almost certainly have lost control and crashed into the ocean.[48]

CHAPTER 4

Is It Possible?

The number of disappearances and odd experiences within the Bermuda Triangle have continued to grow. However, experts do not agree about what causes the disappearances or even the near misses. Since the earliest ships and boats have gone missing or have had unusual experiences within the triangle, people have put forth all sorts of theories on the cause. Some of these ideas seem based at least partially in scientific fact, while some are more speculative.

Sea Monsters?

One of the earliest explanations for disappearances within the triangle is that some sort of sea creature either attacks a ship or somehow becomes entangled in one. One particular creature mentioned by several researchers is the giant squid. And while it may sound far-fetched, the idea of large, aggressive squids has been around for centuries.

Proof is difficult to find, however. In 1896 some thought they had found it. A carcass of what looked like a 200-foot-long (61m) squidlike animal washed up on a beach in St. Augustine, Florida. However, further study found that it was merely part of a whale.

But more interesting evidence has emerged in recent times. In 1985 a ship called the USS *Stein* left port in San Diego, but because its sonar system was not working, it was forced to turn back. After a great deal of searching for the cause of the problem, mechanics discovered it when they looked underneath the ship. The sonar mechanism is contained within a rubber sheath on the underside of the bow. To their astonishment, the sheath was completely shredded. Within the tattered remnants were several huge claws or teeth, which experts believe could have come from a very large squid or shark.

"We Don't Know What Lies Under the Depths of the Ocean"

The idea of a large sea animal attacking and sinking a ship is not limited to as yet unseen creatures like giant squids. Occasionally, even well-known animals that are usually nonthreatening have been known to become instantly—and unexplainably—aggressive.

In 1972 Dougal Robertson and his family were sailing just south of the Bermuda Triangle in their 43-foot-long (13m) sailboat, the *Lucette.* Though the sea seemed very peaceful that day, the Robertsons were terrified as 3 killer whales broke off from a pod of 20 and suddenly rammed their boat. In less than a minute, the *Lucette* had sunk. Though the family had only a tiny life raft to cling to, they were able to survive 36 days before they were rescued.

Although there was a happy ending, sailors familiar with the story were worried. "I think of that darned story of the *Lucette* every time I'm in that area," admits Brian Hennessy, who has sailed

This is the beak of a giant squid. In 1985 the USS Stein left port in San Diego, but because the sonar wasn't working it was forced to turn back. While checking the ship, workers found several huge claws or teeth, which experts believe could have come from a very large squid.

This computer-generated image shows a giant squid. One of the earliest explanations for disappearances within the Triangle is that some sort of sea creature either attacks a ship or somehow becomes entangled in one. One particular creature mentioned by several researchers is the giant squid. While it may sound far-fetched, the idea of large, aggressive squids has been around for centuries.

Dougal Robertson and his family survived 36 days at sea after killer whales destroyed their sailboat.

for 30 years. "I've seen pods of those whales and admired them. But I guess we don't know what can set large animals like that off. For sure they could sink my boat. And who knows what other disappearances happened where [whales] were the cause?"[49]

Bermuda Triangle researcher Rob Simone agrees, saying that no one knows what sorts of sea creatures inhabit those waters. "We don't know what lies under the depths of the ocean," he says. "It could very well be a giant creature that is particular to that part of the ocean. Maybe its food source is contained there, we don't know. But it could explain some of the ships that were mysteriously lost."[50]

The UFO Connection

Even more remarkable than the theory of giant sea creatures is that of unidentified flying objects (UFOs) in the Bermuda Triangle. From his *Gemini 4* space capsule, U.S. astronaut James McDivitt noted an unidentified object flying over the Bahamas at the time that the Flying Boxcar plane disappeared in 1965. And others who have studied the Bermuda Triangle wonder if somehow beings from other planets could be behind some of the disappearances— or at least may have created the strange occurrences many have experienced. They base their idea on the large number of UFOs reported in the triangle each year.

Of course, it is important to note that a UFO is just what its name implies—an object that is unidentified. According to astronomy teacher Mark G. Anderson:

> People always think it has to do with spaceships and little bubble-headed aliens. That isn't the case. It just means we can't say with any certainty what

the object is. Maybe someday one of these UFOs will be identified as a spaceship—you never know. But until then, the object could be one of a hundred things—a bird, a weather balloon, a piece of an old satellite, an odd cloud, a plane, whatever.[51]

J. Manson Valentine, a retired oceanography professor from the University of Miami, says that the number of sightings of UFOs and unidentified submarine objects has long intrigued him, and for nearly 50 years he has been collecting stories from witnesses. "There are many more sightings in this area than at any other place," says Valentine. "There have been many sightings of aircraft that we know are not planes, and undersea craft that we know are not regular submarines."[52]

The View from the *New Freedom*

Some of the stories Valentine has heard have been especially interesting because they come from very reliable witnesses. An example is the story told by Jim Thorne, an expedition leader of an oceanographic vessel called the *New Freedom.* On August 2, 1975, while on the island of Bimini, one of the islands in the Bahamas, Thorne and another crew member were walking on the beach after dinner when they saw what at first seemed like a large star overhead. At least, as Thorne later reported to Valentine, it looked like a star until it began to move closer:

> [The star] seemed to detach itself from the others and come toward us. It hovered directly above us and then moved to the right. It maneuvered first to the right, then to the left, then back again. It

Killer whales have been known to become aggressive on occasion. Some experts think killer whales could be responsible for a few disappearances in the Triangle.

appeared to stop dead in the sky and hover over different parts of the island [Bimini] and sea around it. I would calculate its speed at several thousand miles per hour. It seemed to be bluish-white, and also to vibrate. At the time we thought we heard a buzzing sound, or rather, a sudden oscillation of sound.[53]

Thorne and his companion said that they watched the object for more than three minutes, until it sped away very fast. No reported military tests or unusual airplanes were in the area at the time, and no explanation was ever found.

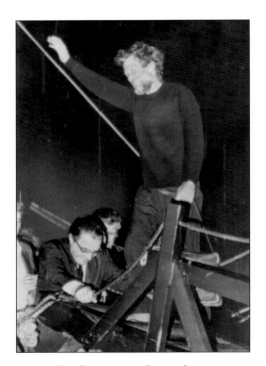

Dougal Robertson, whose ship was sailing just south of the Bermuda Triangle, waves goodbye to the Japanese fishermen who rescued him and his crew after their sailboat was sunk by a pod of killer whales.

"Anything That Happens on the Ship Stays on the Ship"

Though many UFO sightings, like the one in Bimini, are witnessed only by 1 or 2 individuals, a sighting within the Bermuda Triangle in 1971 was far more widespread. It involved the crew of the USS *John F. Kennedy,* one of the navy's large aircraft carriers, and is also especially interesting because the appearance of a UFO coincided with the malfunctioning of important instruments on the ship.

The *John F. Kennedy* had completed a 2-week readiness exercise in the Caribbean and was on its way back to port in Norfolk, Virginia. One sailor recalled that at 20:30 hours (8:30 P.M.) he was below deck in the communications center of the ship, monitoring 8 teletype machines (typewriters that print out telegraphed messages), when he noticed something odd. All of the information coming to the 8 machines was garbled. He walked to the ship's intercom and alerted the ship's control center that there was a problem. He was told that at that time all of the ship's communication hardware was behaving oddly.

Within minutes a frantic call came through the intercom on the bridge that scared those below. They heard someone yell that something was hovering over the ship. Another man frantically screamed that it was the end of the world. The 6 men in the communications center ran up to the flight deck and saw a large object hovering over the ship. It was orange, and they estimated it was between 200 to 300 feet (61 to 91m) in diameter. It was perfectly silent.

Within a few seconds the battle station alerts sounded and the men went back down to the communications center. About 20 minutes later the equipment that had been malfunctioning began working again. The witness reported that though the UFO was seen by everyone, there was no communication sent out to other ships about the incident. In fact, he reports that his commanding officer addressed the crew on the ship's closed-circuit television system, telling them that "anything that happens on the ship stays on the ship."[54]

But Why in the Bermuda Triangle?

As to why the Bermuda Triangle should be visited more than other places is a topic that generates much discussion. Perhaps because it is fairly remote, it offers visitors a way to view the earth without making their presence known to thousands of people, as they would if they visited a large city. Perhaps, as some suggest,

it could be to monitor the way humans use the shipping lanes through the Gulf Stream. By idling their energy sources as they hover over the triangle, they inadvertently may be causing the power outages and equipment malfunctions that seem to occur when UFOs are seen.

Others, such as researcher and 10-year U.S. Air Force veteran John Wallace Spencer, believe there may be a more sinister reason for so many UFOs to visit the triangle. He and others have suggested that the remoteness of the area can give aliens an opportunity to abduct humans—either for experimentation or for observation. Spencer says that such abductions could explain why in most of the disappearances within the triangle, no bodies are ever recovered.

Spencer often has been criticized for the outlandishness of his alien abduction theory, but he has a ready answer in his book *Limbo of the Lost*:

> Since a 575-foot [175m] vessel with 39 crew members disappearing 50 miles [80km] offshore in the Gulf of Mexico and commercial airliners disappearing while coming in for a landing cannot happen according to earthly standards and yet *are* happening, I am forced to conclude that they are actually being taken away from our planet for a variety of reasons.[55]

Too Outlandish a Theory?

Though many are leery of Spencer's alien abduction ideas, some researchers are intrigued by the idea of UFO involvement in the Bermuda Triangle. However, they are more than aware of how they are viewed by the general public. Says Gian Quasar, "Many

Opposite: Large numbers of UFO sightings are reported in the Bermuda Triangle each year, perhaps because it is a fairly remote area. Some people believe that by idling their energy sources as they hover over the triangle, UFOs inadvertently may be causing the power outages and equipment malfunctions that seem to occur when they are seen.

More UFOs are
reported in the
Bermuda Triangle
than anywhere
else on earth.

do not like [to discuss it publicly] because of the erratic behavior the subject often excites today. Discussion of UFOs may elicit giggles from some, scorn from others, derision, dismissal, awe, or even dangerous devotion."[56]

Even so, many believe that the theory of UFOs should be considered. They point to esteemed scientists such as Michio Kaku, a City University of New York professor and one of the world's top physicists. Kaku says that many people dismiss the idea of UFOs (anywhere, not just in the Bermuda Triangle) because humans have not mastered such space travel. On the contrary, he says, the possibility that they are really visitors from another world is too exciting to simply ignore:

> I say, not so fast. . . . You simply cannot dismiss the possibility that some of these UFO sightings are actually sightings of some object created by some advanced civilization—a civilization far out in space, a civilization perhaps millions of years ahead of us in technology. You simply cannot discount that possibility.[57]

"The Sleeping Prophet"

Without a doubt, one of the strangest explanations for the odd occurrences in the Bermuda Triangle has to do not with UFOs but with a psychic named Edgar Cayce. He was known throughout the world as "the Sleeping Prophet" because of the advice he gave while in trances. Much of the advice he gave had to do with diseases that conventional medicine of the day was unable to diagnose or treat. But between 1924 and his death in 1945, Cayce had a great deal to say about the area of the world that today is included within the Bermuda Triangle.

Cayce believed that under part of the Bahamas were the remains of a legendary continent known as Atlantis. There were many stories about Atlantis in ancient times. The first-known mention of it was by the ancient Greek writer Plato in the fourth century B.C, who used the story of Atlantis in some of his writings. According to Plato, Atlantis was a vibrant, progressive civilization thousands of years before, until its citizens became cruel and greedy. To punish them, the gods destroyed the continent with massive explosions, after which Atlantis sank into the sea, never to be seen again.

During several of his trances, Cayce supplied new details about Atlantis. He recounted how technologically advanced its people were and how powerful the empire was. He described the modern roads and pyramids its people had constructed and the explosion that he said had occurred 12,000 years ago. Most interestingly, Cayce predicted during a trance in 1940 that in 1968 or 1969, underwater remains of Atlantis would be discovered "under the slime of ages of seawater—near what is known as Bimini, off the Coast of Florida."[58] Remarkably, it was in 1968, more than 20 years after Cayce died, that evidence was found that perhaps could support his prophecy about Atlantis.

The Bimini Road

The discovery was first viewed from the air by a private pilot, who noticed that the tides near Bimini were moving in a slightly different pattern than usual. As he looked down, he could see an odd rectangular-shaped object—about .25 miles (.40km) in length—just visible under the water. Curious, underwater divers took a closer look and saw that the rectangle was actually a pattern of large stones.

Although some at first thought the stones had fallen there naturally, most scientists agreed that they fit together too precisely to be random. In recent years, researchers have theorized that it was either a road or a wall built by some ancient civilization. Some researchers think that the Bimini Road, as it is often called,

was part of Atlantis, just as Cayce had predicted. And if so, perhaps part of that ancient place below the sea is capable of affecting ships or planes that occasionally fly nearby.

Cayce had also said during one of his trances that Atlantis had depended on crystals for its source of power. People used the

The crew of the USS
John F. Kennedy,
an aircraft carrier,
saw a UFO in the
Bermuda Triangle.

Out of Time?

One unusual theory about the Bermuda Triangle is that something in the area interferes with the passage of time. In the 1996 film *Bermuda Triangle: Secrets Revealed*, pilot Martin Caidin recounts a story of a large U.S. Air Force jet on its way to Bermuda that ran into a bizarre situation:

> "They were at 25,000 feet [7,620m], when the radio operator who had Bermuda on his radar scope noticed that the airplane was no longer moving along the surface of the earth. He called the pilots immediately. . . .

crystals to create massive generators that could utilize the sun's energy to make the energy they needed. Cayce indicated that the Atlanteans had begun misusing the crystals, perhaps creating weapons with them. If so, that might have been the reason the gods became angry and destroyed Atlantis. Some Bermuda Triangle researchers wonder whether some of these crystals still could be underwater interfering with modern navigational instruments.

Now, no one can understand why for 1 hour, with 4 very powerful piston engines, and 2 jets going at full blast, this airplane did not move forward 1 inch. They went lower, they went higher, and nothing they did could make the airplane change position. Until about an hour later they slowly began to leave whatever this force field—we don't really understand what it was. And when they got to Bermuda, they burned about 70 minutes more fuel than they'd ever burned in any other mission between the Azores and Bermuda! And officially on the books, there's no explanation."

"I say, not so fast. . . . You simply cannot dismiss the possibility that some of these UFO sightings are actually sightings of some object created by some advanced civilization."

—Physicist Michio Kaku, discussing UFO reports.

Buildings Under the Water

As far-fetched as such an idea may sound, there is another chapter to the Atlantis–Bermuda Triangle connection. Two years after the discovery of the Bimini Road, physician Ray Brown of Mesa, Arizona, came to Bimini with four friends. The men planned to do some deep-sea diving and hoped to find sunken treasure.

As their boat approached their diving spot, however, they ran

into a violent storm. As Brown explains, "Six to eight foot [1.8 to 2.4m] waves broke over us and we lost most of our equipment. In the morning we saw that our compasses were spinning and our magnetometers were not giving readings." When they finally were able to get to their location, they noticed something odd in the water. "It was murky," Brown says, "but suddenly we could see the outlines of buildings under the water. It seemed to be a large exposed area of an underwater city. We were five divers and we all jumped in and dove down, looking for anything we could find."[59]

"A Crystal Held by Two Metallic Hands"

As Brown and his friends got closer to what appeared to be buildings, the water became clearer. At a depth of 135 feet (41m), Brown says what he saw was amazing:

> I turned to look toward the sun through the murky water and saw a pyramid shape shining like a mirror. Thirty-five to forty feet [11 to 12m] from the top was an opening. I was reluctant to go inside . . . but I swam anyway. The opening was like a shaft debouching into an inner room. I saw something shining. It was a crystal, held by two metallic

hands. I had on my gloves and I tried to loosen it. It became loose. As soon as I grabbed it, I felt this was the time to get out and not come back.[60]

Brown says he has no opinion about the identity of the place he saw underground, except that he is certain that it was an underwater pyramid surrounded by ruins of other buildings. Because he is not certain of the coordinates of the area, it is difficult to determine whether his story is true. Even so, since that time, he has given talks about his adventures in the Bahamas, and he often shows audiences the crystal that he claims to have found there. He says that when one holds the crystal, one feels a throbbing sensation, although he is not sure why. Whether that crystal is an artifact of Atlantis is not known.

No One Knows

There are many interesting possible links between the Bermuda Triangle and UFOs and Atlantis, but scientists and triangle researchers admit that there is little hard evidence to support such theories. Perhaps scientific tests can be done on the stones of the Bimini Road, for example, to determine whether they are old enough to be part of that ancient civilization. Or maybe someday definite proof will establish the existence of alien spacecraft visiting earth or even a mammoth sea creature capable of sinking ships. Until that time, however, these theories have limited value.

CHAPTER 5

Is There a Mystery at All?

While some of the theories put forth to explain the strange happenings in the Bermuda Triangle are intriguing, many people believe the answers lie in less bizarre ideas. The reasons for most of the disappearances may not be as colorful as UFOs and blue holes in the ocean, many experts say, but they are more grounded in logic and scientific possibility.

Rust Buckets

Sometimes, say naval experts, the cause is nothing sinister. Instead, it is merely the fact that so many vessels on the sea are in bad physical shape. They may have specific mechanical problems or may just be so poorly maintained that the slightest stress—a storm, powerful waves—could overcome them.

"A lot of them, even some of the big tankers, are basically rust buckets," says crewman Roland McElroy, a retired seaman who worked on several ships that operate within the area of the Bermuda Triangle. "They've got all kinds of navigation problems, engine problems. A lot of them leak and really need complete overhauling." McElroy says that the expense of overhauling or even repairing such problems can be staggering. "Millions of dollars," he says. "A lot of these companies don't want to spend that kind of money. And to tell you the truth, a lot of the owners ignore it, put it off. Some don't even do routine maintenance. I mean, they do just enough to get by. But they're playing the odds, hoping to get a few more months out of [a ship] before it just goes belly-up."[61]

The *Marine Sulphur Queen*

One of the most vivid examples of such a boat was the *Marine Sulphur Queen,* a 523-foot-long (159m) tanker that carried a crew of 39. It disappeared in February 1963 as it sailed through the Bermuda Triangle on its way from Texas to Norfolk, Virginia. There had been one radio message on February 4 after leaving Texas, but nothing after that. It was listed as missing 2 days later. Though a thorough search was conducted by the Coast Guard, there was no sign of the ship, and many suspected that the *Queen* was another victim of the Bermuda Triangle.

More than a week after the search was called off, however, there was a new development. Some debris was discovered—a fog horn, a few life jackets, and most convincing, a broken piece of wood with part of the ship's name: "arine Sulph." It appeared that the *Queen* had not vanished at all, but rather had sunk for some reason. But it was still puzzling why there had been no distress call, no SOS, from the ship.

"A lot of them, even some of the big tankers, are basically rust buckets."

—Mechanic Roland McElroy, on the poor condition of many ships.

The Coast Guard's board of inquiry, which looks into catastrophic events occurring at sea, conducted a massive investigation to find out as much as possible about why the ship sank. According to one reporter, the mystery "seemed to lie less in the fact that the *Sulphur Queen* had disappeared than in wonderment about how it had ever managed to put to sea in the first place."[62]

"It Looked like an Old Garbage Can Afloat"

The wife of Adam Martin, a seaman who lost his life on that last voyage, said she was struck by how awful the *Marine Sulphur Queen* looked. "I never wanted to be a seaman's wife," she admitted, "but he had to earn a living. I came to see him off. The poor soul. I felt sorry for him when he first saw his new ship. It looked like an old garbage can afloat."[63]

The ship's appearance seemed consistent with its performance. Men who had worked on the boat in the past agreed that it was a firetrap. It was fitted with big tanks with which to transport sulphur—a highly flammable material used to make gunpowder. Crewmen said that the tanks leaked frequently and the sulphur caught fire. Fires on the ship were so commonplace, in fact, that the officers eventually gave up sounding the ship's fire alarm.

Once, the men said, the *Queen* sailed into port in New Jersey with fires still smoking and stinking (burning sulphur smells like rotten eggs), unloaded the cargo, and sailed off again, still on fire. One crewman, known to the men as "Big Brother," said that a young sailor told him, "Big Brother, we are about to burn our house down.[64] Hearing such accounts about the ship, it seems less likely that it was another statistic of unknown forces in the triangle than a victim of its own poor condition—perhaps a sudden explosion at sea, with no time to send out an SOS call.

Human Error

Another logical explanation for ships and planes disappearing within the borders of the Bermuda Triangle is mistakes by captains and pilots. Sometimes the owner of a small boat may ignore reports of ominous weather that could prove life-threatening. A captain may be careless, hitting an object in the water that could cause the boat to sink rapidly. Many familiar with the waters near Bermuda, for example, say that can happen easily because of the turbulence and converging currents of the Gulf Stream within the triangle. And those same rapidly moving waters can cause the evidence of any tragedy to disappear very quickly.

Some U.S. Navy and Coast Guard personnel have been quoted off the record as verifying that some Bermuda Triangle disappearances are indeed mysterious and unexplained. However, the official Coast Guard position is that human mistakes, together with other factors, can explain most of those disappearances—as its 1996 fact sheet maintains: "Not to be underestimated is the human error factor. A large number of pleasure boats travel the waters between Florida's Gold Coast and the Bahamas. All too often, crossings are attempted with too small a boat, insufficient knowledge of the area's hazards, and a lack of good seamanship."[65]

No Mystery at All?

The Coast Guard's official position is seconded by Larry Kusche, who wrote a book in 1986 called *The Bermuda Triangle Mystery—Solved.* Kusche, who compiled dozens of cases of Bermuda Triangle events in his book, uses information he gathered from old newspaper clippings to explain many of them. He maintains that there is no mystery at all—merely a long list of plane crashes and

One ship, the *Marine Sulphur Queen*, had so many fires onboard that the officers stopped sounding the alarm.

sunken ships due to human error, weather events, or malfunctioning instruments.

He lays much of the blame on media sensationalism and insists that much of the Bermuda Triangle research by others has been questionable—or worse. In fact, he writes of Charles Berlitz, the author of a best-selling book on the Bermuda Triangle, "If Charles Berlitz were to report that a boat were red, the chance of it being some other color is almost a certainty."[66]

But Kusche himself is not without his critics. Respected researcher Gian Quasar agrees that while Kusche's research has found errors in some of the Bermuda Triangle cases, he has failed in many others. Kusche, Quasar says, has criticized some of the research, but he has not come up with better reasons for disappearances within the area.

Quasar also maintains that some of Kusche's research is just as shoddy as some of the earlier research that he criticizes. For example, in the case of the USS *Cyclops,* Kusche has relied on incomplete or erroneous newspaper clippings to prove his points. In other cases, he has ignored a great deal of data that might have forced him to make different conclusions. Writes Quasar, "His meticulous research led to his overlooking the 1,500 papers amassed on the *U.S.S. Cyclops* and the ten-year search and investigation contained in . . . the National Archives."[67]

Bubbles from Below?

One thing that has energized discussion about the Bermuda Triangle in recent years has been the emergence of new research that makes some of the earlier theories much more promising. For example, one earlier theory—that was deemed a bit improbable in years past—has to do with a colorless, odorless gas found under the ocean floor. Called methane, it is created when dead sea life (such as plants, fish, and so on) decays.

Methane becomes captured between layers of sediment at the bottom of the ocean. Occasionally, pressure from the increasing amount of gas builds up and bursts through the layers of sediment and bubbles to the surface. For years, researchers suggested that a large amount of methane gas released from the ocean floor might be able to actually sink a boat.

That could conceivably occur because to stay afloat, any ship needs to displace, or push outward, a mass of water that is equal to its own mass. The methane gas would make the water less dense around the ship since it would turn the water to bubbling foam, as Joseph Bishop, an oceanographer from the National Oceanic and Atmospheric Administration explains:

> If a ship was in one of these areas where methane was bubbling at a great rate, what you would get is a density of water that would be decreased 20 or 30 percent, and a ship going through that area would lose buoyancy and sink rapidly. We've actually had offshore oil rigs that have had deposits of gases released, and when these deposits were released, the rigs did sink quite quickly, because the buoyancy of the water was no long there to hold them up.[68]

"There's Evidence to Prove It"

Could methane bubbles explain the sinking of ships within the Bermuda Triangle? A number of new findings have made the theory much more likely. For one, oceanographers have recently

"There's no doubt that [these] methane bubbles could sink a ship."

—U.S. geologist Bill Dillon, on the power of methane bubbles rising from the bottom of the ocean.

Pictured are methane bubbles. Methane, a colorless, odorless gas found under the ocean floor, is created when dead sea life decays. Methane becomes captured between layers of sediment at the bottom of the ocean. Occasionally, pressure from the increasing amount of gas builds up and bursts through the layers of sediment and bubbles to the surface. Researchers have suggested that a large amount of methane gas released from the ocean floor might be able to actually sink a boat.

found that the Bermuda Triangle contains the richest deposits of methane gas on the planet. One researcher, a British oceanographer named Ben Clennell, says that underwater landslides off the coast of Florida may be releasing large amounts of methane from the ocean floor. While Bill Dillon, a U.S. geologist, is not as sure of that as Clennell, he agrees that methane can be extremely dangerous. "There's no doubt," Dillon insists, "that [these] methane bubbles could sink a ship."[69]

Interestingly, some recent experiments have been done on wrecks to try to surmise how a particular ship ended up on the bottom of the ocean. Alan Judd, a marine geologist from England, took a team of researchers to the North Sea to look for wrecks on the ocean floor. He was especially interested in an area called Witch Ground, the site of many circular craters caused by escaping bursts of methane gas. It was there that Judd and his team used a remote-control submarine equipped with powerful cameras and sonar equipment to see if they could locate a wreck below.

After several hours they were excited to discover what seemed to be an old Scottish fishing boat that they estimated had sunk in the 1930s. The 75-foot-long (23m) steel boat was lying at the bottom, directly on top of the largest methane crater, a 492-foot-wide (150m) spot known as Witch's Hole. Judd and his crew were fascinated to see that the boat was in fairly good shape, with surprisingly no damage to the front or back ends. That ruled out the possibility that it had collided with something—one of the biggest causes of shipwrecks. And because it had come to rest exactly on Witch's Hole, Judd believes that the chances were 10,000 to 1 that it had been a victim of the gas bubbles. "For a boat to have randomly landed within Witch's Hole," Judd says, "would be an amazing coincidence."[70]

He also believes that the same phenomenon could be sinking boats within the Bermuda Triangle. He says that such an event would occur very quickly, not giving crew a chance to radio an SOS or even launch a lifeboat. The ship would simply disappear down the hole formed by the gas like an elevator going down a shaft. "Any ship caught above [the methane eruption] would sink," he says. "People jumping overboard in lifejackets would sink, too."[71]

Rogue Waves

Another interesting area of research centers around waves in the area of the Bermuda Triangle. For centuries sailors have told stories about gigantic waves that come out of nowhere and can sink a ship in an instant. But scientists have dismissed such tales as mere legends, much like sea serpents—exciting stories, but totally fiction. Some scientists, such as oceanographer Joseph Bishop once conceded that some of the waves within the triangle could be somewhat bigger than normal during storms, due to the Gulf Stream, although they would be far less scary than the legends described:

> The warm air above the Gulf Stream sort of feeds the storms, so you wind up with waves that might be instead of 10 feet [3m], might be 15 or 18 feet [4.6 or 5.5m]. And in a small boat at night, encountering over a period of fifteen minutes, waves that change from 10 to 18 feet [3 to 5.5m] could really be a disaster, especially if everybody is below deck sleeping.[72]

But the idea of these monster waves was different than this—far larger and more powerful, and in the last several decades, the reports from crews who had encountered such waves had increased. But scientists still were doubtful. Some said that sailors often tended to exaggerate the dangers they face at sea. Others insisted that it was very difficult for a crewman to estimate the height of a wave accurately while on a boat bobbing on the waves.

However, on January 1, 1995, that all changed. An offshore oil platform in the North Atlantic experienced what scientists had not believed was possible—a single huge wave that registered more than 84 feet (26m) according to the platform's laser equipment. And in the years since then, researchers have discovered that those eyewitness accounts were indeed believable—that such monster waves do indeed exist, and that they are larger than anyone had believed possible.

"I . . . Hope I Never Will Meet Such a Monster"

The next giant waves were reported in February 2000, when a large British research ship was fighting through a storm just west of Scotland. Its instruments measured several—some up to 95 feet (29m)—taller than a 9-story building. In their latest research, scientists using computers to simulate the creation of such waves say that the ocean could conceivably form waves 198 feet (60m) tall. That is higher than the Statue of Liberty, say oceanographers, or the Capitol rotunda in Washington, D.C.

Researchers also have learned that though these waves can occur in several regions of the world, they seem most likely to form in places with strong currents, where winds frequently move in the opposite direction. That describes perfectly the area of the

Bermuda Triangle. Researcher Bengt Fornberg says that such currents, just like those of the Gulf Stream, seem to focus waves "like a magnifying glass concentrates sunlight."[73]

The other finding is that the waves are far more common than earlier believed. Research vessels, satellite imagery, and mathematical models done since 2004 have shown that there are, at any given moment, about 10 of these waves forming in the Bermuda Triangle, the North Sea, and other "hot spots" where currents are strong. And not only could they easily swamp a large ship, some concede that these large waves could even swallow a low-flying plane. "I never met, and hope I never will meet, such a monster,"[74] admits German researcher Wolfgang Rosenthal.

No Single Explanation

It is entirely possible that monster waves can explain some of the disappearances in the Bermuda Triangle. And methane gas rising from the ocean floor could have caused some shipwrecks in the triangle, too. But no matter what theory or explanation that is put forward—from pilot error to the nonseaworthiness of many

This computer-generated image shows a monster wave. Researchers have said that these waves most likely form in places with strong currents, where winds frequently move in the opposite direction, like in the Bermuda Triangle.

Tiny Little Methane Eaters

Scientists have learned that if not for an odd bacteria-like organism called archaea, the oceans would have far more methane gas than they already do. In the online article "Great Moments in Science," posted on the ABC.net site, scientist Karl Kruszeinicki says that archaea are amazingly adaptable, "having been around since the first days of life on our planet, about 3.8 billion years ago." They are so adaptable, in fact, that they are able to withstand hotter, saltier water than other life-forms. So when those dead bodies of fish and other sea life float downward onto the ocean floor, the archaea there eat a lot of them up.

That makes less methane and less chance of dangerous methane bubbles. And because methane rising into the atmosphere causes global warming, too, the archaea help the planet. In fact, says Kruszeinicki, "If these little methane eaters didn't exist, there'd be an extra 300 million tons of methane each year bubbling up from the ocean floor."

ships—no single answer can explain the hundreds of disappearances of ships and planes within the triangle.

Even the most diehard believers that there is some mystery about the Bermuda Triangle agree that if even 90 percent of the disappearances occurred because of such logical reasons, that still leaves hundreds of cases where those explanations do not seem to work. What, they wonder, can explain the near misses with exceptionally talented pilots and state-of-the-art equipment and perfect weather?

The answer, to those who believe there is a mystery in the Bermuda Triangle, is to continue to discover answers for individual cases, one by one, rather than to look for a single answer that will explain everything. That is what engineer Graham Hawkes and his exploration ship, *Deep See,* thought they had found while searching for sunken treasure in May 1991.

"Aliver and Weller"

Hawkes and his crew were using a remote operated vehicle (ROV) to search the deep waters 10 miles (16km) off the coast of Fort Lauderdale, Florida, when the ROV's camera showed 5 planes lying along the bottom. The planes were clearly Avengers, the same aircraft flown by the pilots of Flight 19. Hawkes had seen sunken Avengers before, and he did not get too excited until he saw that one of the planes had the number 28 stenciled on its tail—the same number as the lead plane in Flight 19.

That discovery did excite him, but he cautiously explained to the media that it would be necessary to check the serial number of the planes against those of Flight 19's planes before they would know for sure. That would take weeks, however, because there was 45 years' worth of plankton and other growth that must be

cleaned off before the numbers could be read. Even so, the press was ecstatic, for it seemed likely that the long-ago mystery had finally been solved. "This time," *Newsweek* magazine proclaimed, "the Bermuda triangle gives one back."[75]

Over the following weeks the ROV and electronic robots gradually made their way around the wrecks and found the numbers on the other planes, but they could see that those numbers did not match those of the doomed Flight 19. And further research found that the U.S. Navy had often recycled numbers on its planes, so the discovery was a different number 28 Avenger. Military sources guessed that the planes had likely crashed years ago while making practice torpedo runs in the area.

It seemed that the mystery of Flight 19 had not been solved after all. "The Bermuda Triangle, if you want to find mystery," Hawkes told reporters, "is probably even aliver and weller than it was before."[76]

Still a Mystery

Hawke's words were true in 1991, and they are true in the twenty-first century. The unexplained disappearances and bizarre happenings within the triangle continue to occur. Planes continue to vanish, though weather is rarely a factor. Friends and associates of the missing verify how experienced they were and insist that pilot error could not be a factor.

Gian Quasar, probably the most diligent of the modern Bermuda Triangle researchers, believes that science has not explained the mysteries. In fact, he says, the triangle is still as puzzling today as it was a half century ago. "Even with technology like radar and long-range radios, disappearances continue," he says. "Far from solving the mysteries, our modern devices have only confirmed how unusual they are."[77]

Even the skeptics admit that all of the strange occurrences cannot be explained away. And that may be a good thing, says Quasar, for it is mysteries that propel people to ask hard questions. "Mystery is like a guide that leads us to the future of discovery," he says. "It shows us what we do not yet know or understand and must strive to study."[78]

This image is from one of the Deep See's cameras. It shows one of the downed planes the crew discovered and at first believed to be Flight 19.

NOTES

Introduction: Without a Trace

1. Martin Caidin, "The Triangle with Four (or More) Sides," *Fate,* January 1993, p. 49.
2. Quoted in Adi-Kent Thomas Jeffrey, *The Bermuda Triangle.* New Hope, PA: New Hope, 1973, p. 3.
3. Quoted in Jeffrey, *The Bermuda Triangle,* p. 147.
4. Gian Quasar, *Into the Bermuda Triangle: Pursuing the Truth Behind the World's Greatest Mystery.* New York: McGraw-Hill, 2004, p. 1.

Chapter 1: Centuries of Lost Ships

5. Quoted in Charles Berlitz, *The Bermuda Triangle.* New York: Avon, 1974, p. 42.
6. Quoted in Jeffrey, *The Bermuda Triangle,* p. 16.
7. Quoted in *History 41: The American Colonies,* "Christopher Columbus, Journal (1492)," Bruce Dorsey, Swarthmore College, Spring 1999. www.swarthmore.edu.
8. Quoted in Larry Kusche, *The Bermuda Triangle Mystery: Solved.* New York: Warner, 1975, pp. 37–38.
9. Quoted in Quasar, *Into the Bermuda Triangle,* p. 58.
10. Quoted in Bermuda-Triangle.Org, "A Passage to Oblivion: The Disappearance of the U.S.S. *Cyclops.*" www.bermuda-triangle.org.
11. Quoted in Berlitz, *The Bermuda Triangle,* p. 47.
12. Quoted in John Harden, *The Devil's Tramping Ground & Other North Carolina Mystery Stories.* Chapel Hill: University of North Carolina Press, 1949, p. 8.
13. Quoted in Quasar, *Into the Bermuda Triangle,* pp. 68–69.
14. Kusche, *The Bermuda Triangle Mystery,* p. 73.
15. Quoted in Kusche, *The Bermuda Triangle Mystery,* p. 217.
16. Quasar, *Into the Bermuda Triangle,* p. 64.
17. Quasar, *Into the Bermuda Triangle,* p. 82.

Chapter 2: Vanishing from the Air

18. Berlitz, *The Bermuda Triangle*, pp. 12–13.
19. Quoted in Berlitz, *The Bermuda Triangle*, pp. 13–14.
20. Quoted in Quasar, *Into the Bermuda Triangle*, pp. 15–16.
21. Quoted in Quasar, *Into the Bermuda Triangle*, p. 16.
22. Quoted in Tom Post, "The Mystery of the Lost Patrol," *Newsweek*, May 27, 1991, p. 25.
23. Quoted in Post, "The Mystery of the Lost Patrol," p. 25.
24. John Wallace Spencer, *Limbo of the Lost*. New York: Bantam, 1974, p. 33.
25. Quoted in Quasar, *Into the Bermuda Triangle*, p. 24.
26. Berlitz, *The Bermuda Triangle*, p. 25.
27. Quoted in Meg Jones, "Bermuda Triangle Mystery Still Haunts," *Milwaukee Journal Sentinel*, December 17, 2005. www.jsonline.com.
28. Quoted in Jones, "Bermuda Triangle Mystery Still Haunts."
29. Quoted in "*Gemini 4*/Astronaut James McDivitt Sighting of Cylindrical Object in Space." www.ufoevidence.org.
30. Roger Johnson, telephone interview with author, May 6, 2008.

Chapter 3: Near Misses in the Triangle

31. Quoted in Berlitz, *The Bermuda Triangle*, p. 94.
32. Brian Hennessy, telephone interview with author, May 21, 2008.
33. Quoted in Berlitz, *The Bermuda Triangle*, p. 93.
34. Quoted in Berlitz, *The Bermuda Triangle*, p. 93.
35. Quoted in Colin Wilson and Damon Wilson, *Mammoth Encyclopedia of the Unexplained*. New York: Carroll and Graf, 2000, p. 61.
36. Quasar, *Into the Bermuda Triangle*, p. 99.
37. Quoted in Quasar, *Into the Bermuda Triangle*, p. 99.
38. Quoted in Quasar, *Into the Bermuda Triangle*, p. 97.
39. Quoted in Quasar, *Into the Bermuda Triangle*, p. 97.
40. Quoted in John Miller, "Eyewitness in the Bermuda Triangle," *Fate*, January 1993, p. 63.
41. Quoted in Miller, "Eyewitness in the Bermuda Triangle," p. 63.
42. Quoted in Berlitz, *The Bermuda Triangle*, p. 95.
43. Caidin, "The Triangle with Four (or More) Sides," p. 51.
44. Caidin, "The Triangle with Four (or More) Sides," p. 53.
45. Quoted in Quasar, *Into the Bermuda Triangle*, p. 104.
46. Caidin, "The Triangle with Four (or More) Sides," p. 56.

47. Caidin, "The Triangle with Four (or More) Sides," p. 58.
48. Caidin, "The Triangle with Four (or More) Sides," p. 60.

Chapter 4: Is It Possible?
49. Hennessy, interview.
50. Quoted in *Bermuda Triangle: Secrets Revealed*. VHS. Directed by John Wilcox. Chicago: Questar, 1996.
51. Mark G. Anderson, interview with author, August 22, 2008.
52. Quoted in Quasar, *Into the Bermuda Triangle*, p. 112.
53. Quoted in Quasar, *Into the Bermuda Triangle*, p. 113.
54. *UFO Casebook*, August 25, 2008. www.ufocasebook.com.
55. Spencer, *Limbo of the Lost*, p. 136.
56. Quasar, *Into the Bermuda Triangle*, p. 215.
57. Quoted in ABC News, "UFOs: Seeing Is Believing," aired February 24, 2005.
58. Quoted in Biblioteca Pléyades, "Edgar Cayce Predictions." www.biblioteca pleyades.net.
59. Quoted in Amorós Designs, "Dr. Brown's Recovered Crystal." www.fortunecity.com.
60. Quoted in Amorós Designs, "Dr. Brown's Recovered Crystal."

Chapter 5: Is There a Mystery at All?
61. Roland McElroy, telephone interview with author, August 12, 2008.
62. Quoted in *Time*, "The Queen with the Weak Back," March 8, 1963. www.time.com.
63. Quoted in *Time*, "The Queen with the Weak Back."
64. Quoted in *Time*, "The Queen with the Weak Back."
65. U.S. Coast Guard and U.S. Navy, "Bermuda Triangle Fact Sheet," May 1996. www.sartori.com.
66. Quoted in Robert Todd Carroll, "Bermuda (or "Devil's") Triangle," *Skeptic's Dictionary*, August 28, 2008. http://skepdic.com.
67. Quasar, *Into the Bermuda Triangle*, p. 93.
68. Quoted in *Bermuda Triangle: Secrets Revealed*.
69. Quoted in René Ebersole, "Bubble Trouble," *Current Science*, November 9, 2001, p. 10.
70. Quoted in Joanna Marchant, "Swallowing Ships," *New Scientist Space*. http://space.newscientist.com.
71. Quoted in Marchant, "Swallowing Ships."
72. Quoted in *Bermuda Triangle: Secrets Revealed*.

73. Quoted in William J. Broad, "Rogue Giants at Sea," *New York Times*, July 8, 2006. www.nytimes.com.

74. Quoted in Broad, "Rogue Giants at Sea."

75. Post, "The Mystery of the Lost Patrol."

76. Quoted in Tim Golden, "Mystery of Bermuda Triangle Remains One," *New York Times,* June 5, 1991, p. A30.

77. Quasar, "The Bermuda Triangle," *Boys' Life,* June 3, 2003, p. 30.

78. Quasar, "The Bermuda Triangle," p. 30.

FOR FURTHER RESEARCH

Books

Judith Herbst, *Lands of Mystery.* Minneapolis: Lerner, 2005. A very readable book that deals with the mystery of the underwater civilization of Atlantis.

Ann Margaret Lewis, *Atlantis.* New York: Rosen, 2002. This book provides background on the lost continent of Atlantis, with good illustrations and a helpful index.

Rob MacGregor and Bruce Gernon, *The Fog: A Never Before Published Theory of the Bermuda Triangle Phenomenon.* Woodbury, MN: Llewellyn, 2005. This is an interesting account of the theory of magnetic fog, which the authors believe is responsible for disappearances in the Bermuda Triangle.

Dougal Robertson, *Survive the Savage Sea.* Dobbs Ferry, NY: Sheridan House, 2002. This first-person account describes the ordeal of Roberton's family, when killer whales attacked their boat, the *Lucette.*

Gail Stewart, *UFOs.* San Diego: Reference-Point, 2007. This book discusses the various theories of unidentified flying objects as well as famous sightings.

Internet Sources

ABC.net, "Great Moments in Science: Bermuda Triangle 3." www.abc.net.au/science/k2/moments/s1070889.htm.

Jason Dowling, "Bermuda Triangle Mystery Solved? It's a Load of Gas," *Fairfax-Digital,* October 23, 2003. www.theage.com.au/articles/2003/10/22/1066631498889.html.

Megan Sever, "Beneath the Bermuda Triangle," *Geotimes,* November 2004. www.geotimes.org/nov04/geophen.html.

Web Sites

The Bermuda Triangle (http://unex-t.com/thetruth/bermuda.htm). A very readable site that includes explanations from

UFOs and Atlantis to methane bubbles and simple weather changes in the area.

Bermuda-Triangle.org (www.bermuda-triangle.org). Hosted by researcher Gian Quasar, this is a very complete site. It includes texts, reproductions of real documents, and photographs detailing many aspects of individual cases in the Bermuda Triangle.

Bimini: The Road to Atlantis (www.beyondtopsecret.com/BiminiRoad.html). This site has incredible photographs of the stones that make up the fabled Bimini Road.

Flight 19 (www.history.navy.mil/faqs/faq15-2.htm). This is an excellent, detailed account of the disappearance of Flight 19 from the U.S. Navy's point of view, including transmissions from the pilots as well as from rescue planes.

The UnMuseum, "The Bermuda Triangle" (www.unmuseum.org/triangle.htm). From the case of the *Cyclops* to Flight 19, this site looks at the disappearances and odd occurrences from a skeptical point of view.

INDEX

on boundaries of Bermuda Triangle, 7
Consolidated PBY-6A Catalina flight,
    51–55
on time passage irregularities, 72–73
Carroll A. Deering (schooner), 18–20
Catalina flight, 51–55
causes
    electromagnetic fields, 55
    human error, 79–80
    investigations unable to find any
        Flight 19, 29
        "Flying Boxcar"
            disappearance, 35
        Star Tiger, 31, 34
    methane gas, 80–81, 82–83 (illustration),
        83–85
    opinions about, 49, 49 (chart)
    poor condition of ships, 76–78
    rogue waves, 85–87, 87 (illustration)
    sea monsters, 56–57, 58–59 (illustration),
        60, 62–63 (illustration)
    UFOs, 36–38, 60–61, 64–65, 66 (illustra-
        tion), 67–68
    U.S. military explanations, 7, 9
    weather
        fog, 53, 54–55
        turbulence oddities, 43–47, 48, 50, 74
Cayce, Edgar, 68–72
C-119 disappearance, 34–38, 39 (illustration)
Clennell, Ben, 84
Columbus, Christopher, 12, 13 (illustration)
compass malfunctions, 12, 26, 28, 74
Consolidated PBY-6A Catalina flight, 51–55
Continental Airlines jet, 46–47
Cox, Robert, 27–28
crystals, 72, 75

D

Deep See (exploration ship), 89, 91 (illustra-
    tion)
Deering (schooner), 18–20
Dillon, Bill, 82, 84
distress calls
    absence of
        Marine Sulphur Queen, 77
        Martin Mariner and, 28–29
        USS *Cyclops*, 16
    sent by
        Flight 19, 27
        Witchcraft, 20
Durant, Robert, 42–43

E

electrical oddities, 41–42, 43
electromagnetic fields, 55
electronic equipment. *See* specialized equip-
    ment
equipment. *See* specialized equipment

F

fire ball, 12
Flight 19 disappearance, 25–29, 32–33 (illus-
    tration), 36–37, 89–90
flying blind, 48
"flying boat" experience, 51–55
"Flying Boxcar" disappearance, 34–38, 39
    (illustration)
fog, appearance of, 53, 54–55
Fornberg, Bengt, 87
fuel gauge malfunctions, 42

monster waves, 85–87, 87 (illustration)
Moore, Joe, 46–47

names, 6, 10
navigational equipment. *See* specialized
    equipment
New Freedom (oceanographic vessel), 61, 64
Newsweek (magazine), 90

people missing
    aliens abducted, 67
    Deering crew, 18, 19
    Flight 19 crew, 28
    "Flying Boxcar" crew and passengers, 35
    ghost ships, 23
    HMS *Atlanta* crew, 14
    increasing number of, 9
    Martin Mariner crew, 29
    number of (1945-1975), 6
    Star Ariel crew and passengers, 34
    Star Tiger crew and passengers, 29, 31
    USS *Cyclops*, 15
    Witchcraft sailors, 23
Plato, 69
Powers, Charles, 26
Puerto Rico Trench, 50
pyramid underwater, 74–75

Quasar, Gian
    on absence of signs of ships that disap-
        peared, 23

    on Flight 19 disappearance, 36–37
    on Kusche as researcher, 80
    on mysterious nature of area, 9
    on solving mystery of Bermuda Triangle,
        91
    on turbulence encountered by Macone,
        45
    on UFOs, 67–68
    on *Witchcraft*, 22

Raymond, Andy, 47–48, 50
Robertson, Dougal, 57, 60, 64 (illustration)
rogue waves, 85–87, 87 (illustration)
Rosenthal, Wolfgang, 87
rust buckets, 76–78

Sampson, Osbee, 35
Sanderson, Ivan, 19
Sargasso Sea, 10–12, 11 (illustration), 21
sea monsters, 11, 56–57, 58–59 (illustration),
    60, 62–63 (illustration)
Sea of Lost Ships, 6
Sea of Oblivion, 6
ship disappearances
    absence of signs of wrecks, 14, 23
    annual average since 1975, 6
    distress calls and, 16, 20, 77
    instantaneous nature of, 9
    nineteenth century, 13–15
    number (1945-1975), 6
    twentieth century, 15–20, 22–23, 77–78
Simone, Rob, 60

ABOUT THE AUTHOR

Gail B. Stewart is the author of more than 200 books for young adults. She lives in Minneapolis with her husband, 2 dogs, and a cat. She is the mother of 3 grown sons and is a diehard fan of Gustavus Adolphus College's men's soccer team.